Practical SAS Programming
For Beginners

Lillian Ren

Preface

Through many years as a statistician and data analyst, I've noticed the importance of learning SAS programming in a simple and practical way. When learning and using a new coding language, however, there are so many components to focus on and utilize.

This book presents a high-level, foundational skills to SAS programming with useful tips and is very practical for a real work environment.

Readers should be able to handle an entry level statistical programming or SAS programming job with great confidence after finishing the book and comprehending its contents.

Happy programming!

Lillian Ren

Acknowledgements

Many thanks to my daughter Janet for her inspiration and support of writing this book!

Contents

Chapter 5 Macro

Chapter 6 Array

Chapter 7 System time

Chapter 8 Format and Label

Chapter 9 Data manipulation

Chapter 10 Basic statistical procedures

Chapter 11 Data management and automation setup

Chapter 1

Introduction

As data is the driving force of all areas in our society, the demand for data analysis has grown dramatically and will keep increasing over the years.

SAS is a statistical software suite developed by SAS Institute for advanced analytics, business intelligence, criminal investigation, data management, and predictive analytics.

The output, code, data analysis for this book was generated using SAS software. Copyright © SAS Institute Inc. SAS and all other SAS Institute Inc. product or service names are registered trademarks or trademarks of SAS Institute Inc., Cary, NC, USA.

SAS is a very popular statistical programming platform. The beginners can get started from SAS studio online account. Please follow the instructions to register an account.

http://support.sas.com/ondemand/manuals/SASStudio.pdf

Please click on the following link : https://welcome.oda.sas.com/

A webpage with the following instructions will pop up.

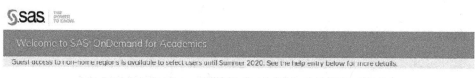

Select your home region and click the desired action below to get started.

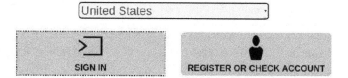

Select the region and click on the sign in button to login .

From the screen shown above, we will be able to access the SAS studio online:

Click on SAS Studio, we can create and run our first SAS program.

The first thing you should do is to create a new folder under the home directory in SAS studio.

- Right click on Files(Home)
- Select new folder
- Type folder name and then click OK. We have successfully created a new folder 'Project' and subfolder 'TEMP'. The folder name can be changed as needed.

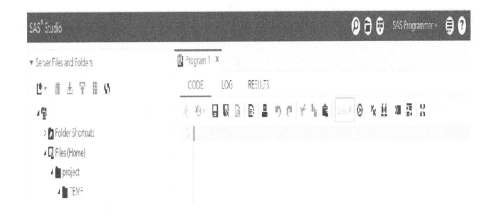

We can write SAS codes under the 'Code' section. We can check the errors after we run our SAS codes within the 'LOG' section. If the SAS codes run successfully, we will be able to see the output of our data in the 'RESULTS' section.

Let's start to write our first SAS codes.

After we created our own folder under File(Home) directory, we can go under the "Server Files and Folders", click on the first tab, the drop down list will show as below:

1. Write our SAS codes

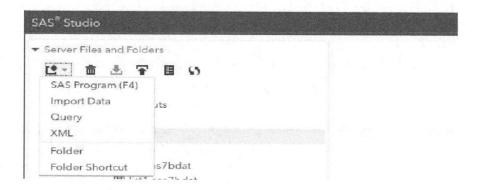

Select **SAS Program(F4)** or click **F4**, the programming window will show up on the right of the screen.

2. Run SAS codes

Under 'CODE' tab, copy the following codes to the screen window and hit the run button:

```
data balance;
   input AccountNumber $ Week1 Week4;
   Balance=Week1-Week4;
   datalines;
2477 195  163
2431 220  198
2456 173  155
2412 135  116
;
proc print data = balance ;
run;
```

Click the run button (a little running icon), we will get the screen below:

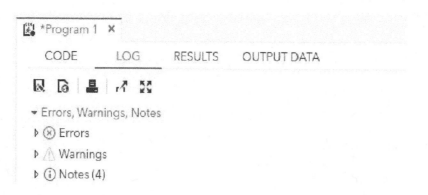

```
 3
 4  data balance;
 5     input AccountNumber $ Week1 Week4;
 6     Balance=Week1-Week4;
 7     format date date9.;
 8     datalines;
 9  2477 195   163
10  2431 220   198
11  2456 173   155
12  2412 135   116
13  ;
14  proc print data = balance ;
15  run;
```

3. Check errors

Click on the 'LOG' tab, we can check whether there is any error from the codes we just submitted.

In this example, there are no errors or warnings but there are four notes which are the descriptions of the data set we just created. If we extend the notes, we can see the following screen:

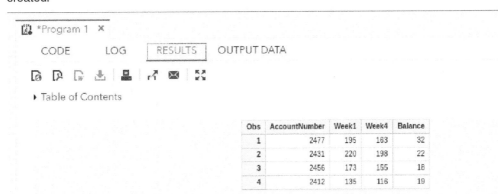

▲ ⓘ Notes (4)

NOTE: The data set WORK.BALANCE has 4 observations and 4 variables.

NOTE: DATA statement used (Total process time):

NOTE: There were 4 observations read from the data set WORK.BALANCE.

NOTE: PROCEDURE PRINT used (Total process time):

*Tips: If there is no number shown for 'Errors' or 'Warnings' in SAS studio, this means that there is no error for the SAS codes. In other SAS versions like SAS 9.4, we can search 'Errors:' or 'Warnings' in the log section.

4. Check results

When clicking on the 'RESULTS' tab, we can see the contents of the SAS dataset we just created.

*Program 1 ✕

CODE   LOG   RESULTS   OUTPUT DATA

▶ Table of Contents

Obs	AccountNumber	Week1	Week4	Balance
1	2477	195	163	32
2	2431	220	198	22
3	2456	173	155	18
4	2412	135	116	19

Yeah! We just successfully coded our first SAS program!

Tips: Remember to save the codes all the time or save as in different versions to avoid overriding the old one.

5. Additional information

We can check more information about our SAS dataset in the 'OUTPUT' section.

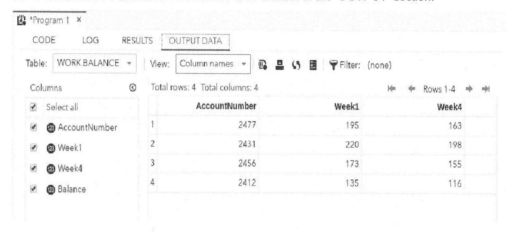

Chapter 2

Basic about SAS programming

1. Data set and variable name conventions

We create SAS dataset with variables. SAS has the following data set and variable name conventions:

1. SAS variable names may be up to 32 characters in length.

2. The first character must begin with an alphabetic character or an underscore.

3. A variable name may not contain blanks.

4. A variable name may not contain any special character other than the underscore or hyphen.

5. A variable can't have the names of special SAS automatic variables (such as _N_ and _ERROR_) or variable list names (such as _NUMERIC_, _CHARACTER_, and _ALL_).

2. Arithmetic and logical operators used in SAS

1) Arithmetic operators

Symbol	Definition	Example	Result
**	exponentiation	a**3	raise A to the third power
*	multiplication	2* X	multiply 2 by the value of X
/	division	Y / 6	divide the value of Y by 6
+	addition	C +D	add D to the value of C
-	subtraction	A – B	subtract the value of B from the value of A

3. Logical operators

Symbol	Expression	Definition	Example
=	EQ	equal to	A = B
^=	NE	not equal to	A ne 8
>	GT	greater than	C > 5
<	LT	less than	D < 6
>=	GE	greater than or equal to	E >= 300
<=	LE	less than or equal to	G <= 100
	IN	equal to one of a list	H in (3, 4, 5)

4. Store data set

When we create a SAS data set, there are two places to go.

- One is a temp data set stored by default in the work library, which will be deleted automatically after you log out of your SAS session.

- We can create permanent data sets by saving data in the user defined library. A user defined SAS library is a folder located on a user's disk drive or on your cloud folder. SAS libraries allow users to safely store data sets and user-defined formats so that they can be accessed without having to reload or re-read them from an external file every time SAS is started. The downside of a user defined library can eat up a lot of storage space on your computer or your cloud space so only use user defined libraries when necessary.

5. How to define a library

We use the LIBNAME statement to create a new SAS library with SAS code.

To create a SAS library, we use the LIBNAME statement as follows:

libname mydata 'c:/folders/myfolders/';

Mydata is the name of the SAS library and it must follow the following conventions:

The name convention of library:

- Limited to eight characters.
- Must begin with a letter or underscore.

- Blanks are not allowed. You usually submit a LIBNAME statement at the beginning of your codes.

A LIBNAME statement consists of

- Libname statement

- Library name and the physical location of the library

- Semicolon

Following the name of the SAS library is the physical location of the SAS library, in this example, it is c:/folders/myfolders/. As you can see in the example above, the physical location of the library must be in quotes and then followed by a semicolon.

Remember that you only need to submit a LIBNAME statement only once during a SAS session.

You might be wondering how to get the physical location of the folder in SAS studio? It is very similar to how we get the physical location of a folder in the PC.

Right click on the folder then select property.

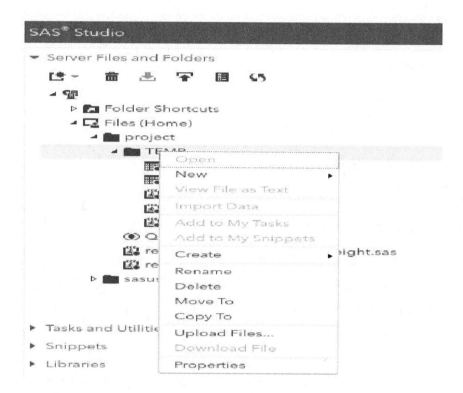

Here is the **Folder Properties**:

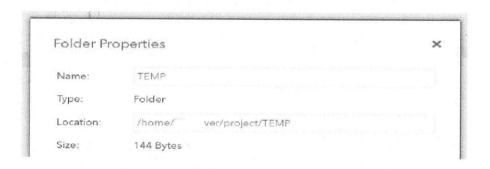

From the location folder, we can get the physical location of the folder.

In order to create a library, you should assign a physical location of a folder. The following LIBNAME statement assigns the mydata libref to my folder.

libname mydata 'c:/folders/myfolders/';

Example 1: create a permanent data set in your folder

```
LIBNAME mydata  '/home/ver/project/TEMP'   ;

data mydata.list;

  input @01 employee_id   6.
        @08 last_name       $10.
        @19 birthday        date7.;

  format employee_id       6.
         last_name         $10.
         birthday          date7.;
datalines;

1245 Carcia    04APR94
1278 Grace     23APR96
1005 Kate      06OCT88
1024 Mike      17JUN03
;
run;
```

After we ran these codes, we created a sas dataset **list.sas7bdat**.

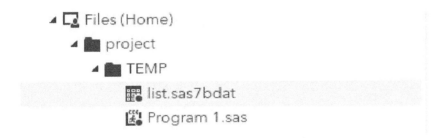

Example 2: Create a temperate data set without being assigned to a library.

*The temperate data set is gone when you close your SAS session;

```
data balance;
  input AccountNumber $ Week1 Week4;
  Balance=Week1-Week4;
  datalines;
2477 195  163
2431 220  198
2456 173  155
2412 135  116
;

proc print data = balance ;
run;
```

Obs	AccountNumber	Week1	Week4	Balance
1	2477	195	163	32
2	2431	220	198	22
3	2456	173	155	18
4	2412	135	116	19

Example 3

Let's create a permanent data set from example 2.

Just type or copy the following codes to SAS session after the you run the example 2

```
LIBNAME mydata '/home/llll12river/project/TEMP';

data mydata.balance;
set balance;
run;
```

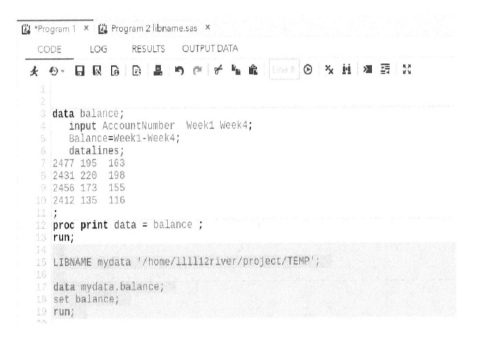

You can see that data set 'balance' is created in folder:

6. SAS data type

6.1. SAS has only two data types: numeric data type and fixed length character strings.
Dates and times are internally stored as numbers.

Character values must be quoted. Missing numeric value In SAS dataset is shown as a dot
(.) and a missing character value is shown as blank. For the following data , the maker AB
has missing data for model and maker AC has missing data for price.

Obs	maker	model	mpg	weight	price
1	AM	CON	22	2930	4090
2	AC	PAC	17	3350	.
3	AB		22	2645	3699
4	BK	CRY	20	3250	4836
5	BN	ELA	16	4089	7825

Macro variables are always characters. Please go to chapter 5 for more information regarding
Macro variables.

6.2. Converting SAS variable types using PUT() or INPUT() function:

When to use put() or input(), you can use the following rules:

PUT() always creates character variables, INPUT() always takes character source variables.

INPUT() can create character or numeric variables based on the informat.

The source format must match the source variable type in PUT().

The source variable type for INPUT() must always be character variables.

Source variable	Target variable	Function	Raw Value	Returned value
Character, Character format	Character	PUT(name, $6.);	Kate	'Kate ' (length will be 6 instead of 5)
Numeric, numeric format	Character	PUT(age, 4.);	30	'30 ' (Length will be 4 instead of 2)
Character, character format	Character	INPUT(agechar, $4.);	'15'	'15' (Length will be 4 instead of 2)
Character,numeric format	Numeric	INPUT(agechar, 4.);	'20'	20

Chapter 3

Creating SAS data sets

We can create SAS data sets in mainly three ways: Data step, import procedure, infile statement.

1. Creating data set from scratch using SAS data step

1.1 Input with data line

```
DATA inventory;
INPUT maker $ model $ mpg weight price;
CARDS;
AM CON 22 2930 4090
AC PAC 17 3350 4849
AB SPI 22 2645 3699
BK CRY 20 3250 4836
BN ELA 16 4089 7825
;
RUN;

PROC PRINT DATA = inventory ;
RUN;
PROC PRINT DATA  = inventory (OBS=2);
RUN;
```

You can also use DATALINES instead of CARDS since there is no significant difference between the two. CARDS is defined as an alias of DATALINES.

Tips: When using the **proc print** statement to check data, you can use **obs = number** to display limited data rows especially for big data sets. It will cause server freeze if you accidentally run this print procedure for a big data set. The whole process will cause you not to be able to save your SAS codes, which will be a very painful experience, especially if you coded a lot. Therefore, it will be a good idea to save your code constantly.

Tips: As we mentioned in chapter 2 that a user defined library can take a lot of storage space on our computer or cloud server space, we usually use the default **WORK library** to store data temporarily.

Here is the screen shot of default libraries in SAS:

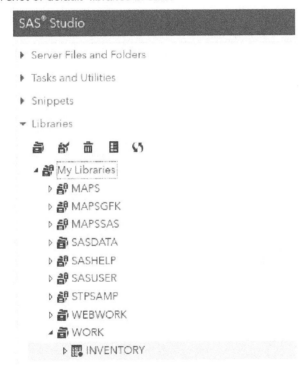

Under **My Libraries**, there are many default libraries created by SAS. You can use datasets in **SASHELP** and **SASDATA** to practice. The detailed usage of other SAS libraries can be found on SAS official website.

If you pay attention to **My Libraries**, you should find the **WORK** library, which is the default library to temporarily store all your data generated by your SAS codes. You can see the '**INVENTORY**' data set is already there. This data set will be gone when you exit the SAS session.

1.2 Get a new data set from an existing SAS dataset

If you want to store the '**INVENTORY**' data set permanently, you should already know how to do it.
Yes, use a user defined library.
If you submit the following codes, you will see that '**INVENTORY**' data set is in your library '**Mydata**'.

1.2.1 Using data step:

```
LIBNAME mydata '/home/ver/project/TEMP';
data mydata.inventory;
set inventory;
run;
```

1.2.2.Using proc sql:

```
proc sql;
create table mydata.inventory as
select * from inventory;
quit;
```

You can also create an identical data set, or subdataset in the WORK library .

```
data inventory_1;
set inventory;
run;
proc print data = inventory_1 ;
run;

data inventory_2;
set inventory;
where maker = 'BK';
run;
proc print data = inventory_2 ;
run;
```

Obs	maker	model	mpg	weight	price
1	AM	CON	22	2930	4090
2	AC	PAC	17	3350	4849
3	AB	SPI	22	2645	3699
4	BK	CRY	20	3250	4836
5	BN	ELA	16	4089	7825

Obs	maker	model	mpg	weight	price
1	AM	CON	22	2930	4090
2	AC	PAC	17	3350	4849
3	AB	SPI	22	2645	3699
4	BK	CRY	20	3250	4836
5	BN	ELA	16	4089	7825

Obs	maker	model	mpg	weight	price
1	BK	CRY	20	3250	4836

We can see that **INVENTORY** and **INVENTORY_1** are identical.

IVENTORY_2 is the only subdataset of Inventory.

2. Using proc import

It is a very common and easy way to prepare data or use existing excel, text or CSV files.

Tips: It's a great idea to comment on your codes.

You can use * ; or /* */ to comment out codes or notes for future reference.

23

You should upload a data file from your computer if you use SAS studio. If SAS has been installed in your computer then you just need to get the file location.

Right click on the file you just uploaded,you can get the file location from the file property.

2.1 Import CSV file

```
proc import datafile = '/home/ver/Client.csv'
      dbms =csv
      out= work.client_csv;
```

```
        getname = yes;
run;
proc print data = client_csv;
run;
```

Obs	CaseNumber	Gender	Age
1	1	F	57
2	2	F	64
3	3	M	64
4	4	M	57
5	5	M	47
6	6	M	21
7	7	M	60
8	8	M	74
9	9	M	40
10	10	M	86
11	11	F	72
12	12	M	49
13	13	M	82
14	14	F	60
15	15	M	75
16	16	M	40
17	17	F	59
18	18	M	82
19	19	F	62

SAS import procedure will automatically assign the data type to your data . You can use **proc contents** to check it out:

```
proc contents data = client_csv; run;
```

Alphabetic List of Variables and Attributes					
#	Variable	Type	Len	Format	Informat
3	Age	Num	8	BEST12.	BEST32.
1	CaseNumber	Num	8	BEST12.	BEST32.
2	Gender	Char	1	$1.	$1.

You can also specify the delimiter, if it is a comma **,** or others like pipe **|** or double **||** or other delimiters.

For example, you can import the same CSV file using the following codes:

Remember to get the right file path from the property of the file.

```
proc import datafile = '/home/myfolder/Client.csv'
        dbms =dlm
        out= work.client_csv_1  replace;
        delimiter = ',';
run;
proc print data = client_csv_1; run;
```

The Print Procedure

Data Set WORK.CLIENT_CSV_1

Obs	CaseNumber	Gender	Age
1	1	F	57
2	2	F	64
3	3	M	64
4	4	M	57
5	5	M	47
6	6	M	21
7	7	M	60
8	8	M	74
9	9	M	40
10	10	M	86
11	11	F	72
12	12	M	49
13	13	M	82
14	14	F	60
15	15	M	75
16	16	M	40
17	17	F	59
18	18	M	82
19	19	F	62

2.2 Import excel file

```
proc import datafile = '/home/ver/product.xls'
dbms =xls
out= work.Product_xls;
getnames = yes;
run;
proc print data = Product_xls; run;
```

Obs	UnitNumber	Product	Total
1	1	F1	134
2	2	F2	264
3	3	M1	342
4	4	M2	157
5	5	M3	247
6	6	M4	121
7	7	MC	160
8	8	MW	574
9	9	MV	340
10	10	M5	586
11	11	FG	272
12	12	KM	1249
13	13	SM	982
14	14	FN	360
15	15	MD	575

We can use **proc contents** to check the data type of the dataset: Product_xls:

```
proc contents data = Product_xls;
run;
```

Alphabetic List of Variables and Attributes					
#	Variable	Type	Len	Format	Informat	Label
2	Product	Char	11	$11.	$11.	Product
3	Total	Num	8	BEST11.		Total
1	UnitNumber	Num	8	BEST11.		UnitNumber

2.3 Import txt file

```
proc import datafile = '/home/ver/case.txt'
dbms =tab
out= work.case_txt;
getnames = yes;
run;
proc print data = case_txt;
run;
```

Obs	CaseNumber	type	total
1	1	AP	40
2	2	IN	40
3	4	AP	40
4	6	NN	40
5	8	PR	21
6	11	PE	21

Use **proc contents,** you can see the variable type, length,format and informat:

Format and informat in SAS:

Format or a variable is how you tell **SAS** to display the values in the variable which show how you will see it.

Informat is declared when you are reading in data or creating a new variable in a data step, the **format** statement can be used in either a data step or a proc sql step.

Alphabetic List of Variables and Attributes					
#	Variable	Type	Len	Format	Informat
1	CaseNumber	Num	8	BEST12.	BEST32.
3	total	Num	8	BEST12.	BEST32.
2	type	Char	2	$2.	$2.

3. Use Infile statement

When we use import procedure, SAS automatically assigns the data type, data length and data format to the data set. However, you can specify the data type, data length, format and informat.

Tips: Always add the IGNOREDOSEOF option to the INFILE statement to avoid possible runtime errors. SAS studio seems not to allow IGNOREDOSEOF option but it works perfectly in SAS 9.4 and later version. IGNOREDOSEOF was commented out here using /* */. You can remove the comment by just deleting /* */.

You don't have to specify a library if you use default library work.

You can change the format,informat and the length of the variables in the **INFILE** statement but you can not make these changes using **proc import**.

3.1 Import txt file using infile statement

```
data case_txt1 ;
  infile '/home/myfolder/case.txt' delimiter='09'x MISSOVER DSD /*IGNOREDOSEOF*/
lrecl=32767 firstobs=2 ;
  informat CaseNumber best12. ;
  informat type $4. ;
  informat total best12. ;
  format CaseNumber best12. ;
  format type $4. ;
  format total best12. ;
  length CaseNumber 6
      total 6
      type $4.;
  input
  CaseNumber
  type $
  total ;
run;
proc print data = case_txt1(obs =10); run;
```

Obs	CaseNumber	type	total
1	1	AP	40
2	2	IN	40
3	4	AP	40
4	6	NN	40
5	8	PR	21
6	11	PE	21

```
proc contents  data = case_txt1;
run;
```

	Alphabetic List of Variables and Attributes				
#	Variable	Type	Len	Format	Informat
1	CaseNumber	Num	6	BEST12.	BEST12.
3	total	Num	6	BEST12.	BEST12.
2	type	Char	4	$4.	$4.

You can see that the length,format and informat for 'CaseNumber' and 'total' have been changed from 8, BEST32.,BEST32, to 6, BEST12, BEST12 respectively.

The length,format and informat for character variable 'Type' have been changed from from 2, $2,$2 to 4, $4.,$4. respectively.

Tips: The default length of a numeric variable in SAS is 8, which is 8 bytes and can store up to 16 digits for a numeric variable in SAS. Therefore, changing the length of a numeric variable is not common. However, when you try to convert a numeric variable to a character variable using the put() function, remember to always use **COMPRESS()** function over the **PUT()** function to remove the possible extra space.

3.2 Import CSV file using infile statement

```
data case_CSV_2 ;

  infile '/home/myfolder/project/TEMP/case.csv' delimiter='|' MISSOVER DSD
/*IGNOREDOSEOF*/      lrecl=32767 firstobs=2 ;

  informat CaseNumber best12. ;
  informat type $4. ;
  informat total best12. ;

  format CaseNumber best12. ;
  format type $4. ;
  format total best12. ;

  length CaseNumber 6
       total 6
       type $4.;

  input
  CaseNumber
  type $
  total  ;

run;
```

Note: The delimiter for this example is pipe '|'. You can also change based on the file you get for the delimiter.

33

3.2 Get data set from database like Microsoft Access, Oracle Database,Microsoft SQL database or mySQL database

We can access other database directly using SAS connection function.

3.2.1 Connect to Oracle Database

```
LIBNAME OracSAS ORACLE USER=&UserNm PASS=&PassWd PATH='EDWP'
SCHEMA=IDWE CONNECTION=GLOBAL;
PROC SQL;
CONNECT USING OracSAS AS OracDB;
/* CODE */
 DISCONNECT FROM OracDB;
 QUIT;
```

3.2.2 Connect to MS SQL Server

```
libname SQLSRVR odbc noprompt = "server=SQLServerName;DRIVER=SQL
Server Native Client 11.0;Trusted Connection=yes" DATABASE = MyDatabase
schema = dbo;

proc sql;
create table dataset1 as
select  var1, var2, var3  from  SQLSRVR.tablename;
quit;
```

3.2.3 Connect to MySQL

```
libname mysqllib mysql user = username  password= password database=mysqldb
server=mysrv1 port=9876;
proc print data=mysqllib.employees;
  where dept='CSR010';
run;
```

3.2.4 Connect to Microsoft Access

If you have SAS/Access Interface to PC Files you may be able to get to the data with a libname statement,which would look like

```
Libname yourlib "C:\pathtoaccessdatabase\MyDatabase.accdb";
```
or
```
Libname yourlib ACCESS Path="C:\pathtoaccessdatabase\MyDatabase.accdb";
```

3.2.4.1 Import a Microsoft Access 2007 Database Table to a SAS Data Set

```
PROC IMPORT OUT=CUSTOMER
DATATABLE='Customers'
DBMS=ACCESS REPLACE;
DATABASE=yourlib;
USEDATE=YES;
SCANTIME=NO;
DBSASLABEL=NONE;
RUN;
```

You can also use SAS/ACCESS Interface to PC Files to read data from PC files for use in SAS reports or applications. You can use SAS data sets to create PC files in various formats. SAS/ACCESS Interface to PC Files includes accessing data in Microsoft Access database files and Microsoft Excel workbook files as well as in other PC file formats.

```
LIBNAME adb 'C:\PCFData\Demo.accdb';
LIBNAME xdb 'C:\PCFData\Demo.xlsx';
```

3.2.4.2 Export a SAS Data Set to Create a Microsoft Access Database File

```
X 'DEL c:\temp\test2000.mdb';
PROC EXPORT DATA=SDF.EMPLOYEE
OUTTABLE='Employees'
DBMS=ACCESS REPLACE;
DATABASE='c:\temp\test2000.mdb';
RUN;
```

3.2.4.3 Export a SAS Data Set to a Microsoft Access Database Table on a SAS PC Files Server

```
PROC EXPORT DATA=SDF.ORDERS (DROP=SPECINST)

OUTTABLE='Orders'

DBMS=ACCESSCS REPLACE LABEL;

DATABASE='c:\temp\testpcfs.mdb';

SERVER="&server";

VERSION=97;

DBDSOPTS='INSERTBUFF=25';

RUN;
```

Chapter 4

Export data

When a dataset has been created, there are different ways to export data. We can export data as excel file, csv file or text file.

1. Export to text file

```
proc export
  data=sashelp.prdsale
  dbms=tab
  outfile="c:\temp\prdsale.txt"   replace;
run;
```

2. Export to CSV file

2.1. Default delimiter comma (,)

```
proc export
  data=sashelp.prdsale
  dbms=csv
  outfile="c:\temp\prdsale.csv"   replace;
run;
```

2.2. Delimiters other than comma (;) ;

For example pipe (|) , semicolon (:) or combined delimiters (; |).

When the delimiter is not comma, you just need to specify the delimiter for '**dbms**' in the proc export session.

```
proc export

  data=sashelp.prdsale

  dbms=dlm delimiter=';'

  outfile="c:\temp\prdsale.csv"   replace;

run;
```

3. Export data to excel file format

```
proc export

  data=s.sale

  dbms=xlsx

  outfile="c:\temp\sale.xlsx"   replace;   run;


proc export

  data=s.sale

  dbms=xls

  outfile="c:\temp\sale.xls"

  replace;   run;
```

4. Output data using SAS Output Delivery System (ODS)

- SAS output, including Statistics, tables, maps, and charts, can be routed to HTML, PDF, RTF, Excel and other file types.

- Output can be used for presentations, reports, and informal data sharing.

- SAS output can be routed to PDF, HTML, RTF, Excel, and other file types using ODS, the Output Delivery System.

To use ODS, you will need to know:

- The proper ODS destination name can be PDF, HTML, and RTF which are commonly used destinations.

- The location, name, and proper file-extension of the file you plan to create.

Tips: This process does not transfer the data sets, only the output results.

ODS output statement

The basic syntax for using the ODS statement in SAS is:

ODS output type

PATH "C:\your folder"

FILE = filename

STYLE = stylename;

PROC some procedure;

ODS output CLOSE;

4.1 Output HTML file:

Create a html file in the home folder with **proc print** output and average weight by maker.

```
LIBNAME mydata '/home/ver/project/TEMP';

ODS HTML

  PATH = '/home/llll12river/project/TEMP'
  FILE = 'Inventory.html'
  STYLE = EGDefault;

proc print data = mydata.Inventory;
run;

proc sql;
select maker,mean(weight)as Ave_weight
from mydata.Inventory
group by maker;
quit;

ODS HTML CLOSE;
```

If you click on the inventory.hml in the folder, you will open a html page with the following tables.

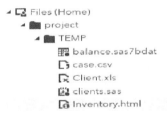

Obs	maker	model	mpg	weight	price
1	AM	CON	22	2930	4090
2	AC	PAC	17	3350	4849
3	AB	SPI	22	2645	3699
4	BK	CRY	20	3250	4836
5	BN	ELA	16	4089	7825

maker	Ave_weight
AB	2645
AC	3350
AM	2930
BK	3250
BN	4089

4.2 Output PDF file

```
LIBNAME mydata '/home/project/TEMP';

ods pdf file= '/home/llll12river/project/TEMP/Inventory.pdf';

proc print data = mydata.Inventory;

run;

proc sql;

select maker,mean(weight)as Ave_weight

from mydata.Inventory

group by maker;

quit;

ods pdf close;
```

4.3 Output Excel file

```
ods excel file= '/home/llll12river/project/TEMP/Inventory.xls';

proc print data = mydata.Inventory;
run;

proc sql;
select maker,mean(weight)as Ave_weight
from mydata.Inventory
group by maker;
quit;

ods excel close;
```

4.4 Output rtx file

```
LIBNAME mydata '/home/llll12river/project/TEMP';

ods rtf file= '/home/llll12river/project/TEMP/Inventory.rtf';
proc print data = mydata.Inventory;
run;

proc sql;
select maker,mean(weight)as Ave_weight
from mydata.Inventory
group by maker;
quit;

ods rtf close;
```

You can see that pdf and rtf files are created.

5. Create a Data Grid Like VB.NET for excel file

You can create a data grid like **VB.NET** in base SAS.

Tableeditor.tpl is a custom tagset that is created by the **TEMPLATE** procedure. The tableeditor tagset

uses HTML, CSS, JavaScript, and the Markup language. You can easily export the output to Excel or other

filetypes.

The most useful use of Tableeditor.tpl is to create a pivot table while exporting your report.

5.1 Get the data file

```
/*Include the TableEditor taget set to create pivot table*/

filename output url

"http://support.sas.com/rnd/base/ods/odsmarkup/tableeditor/tableeditor.tpl";

%include output;

%let dt=%sysfunc(putn(%sysfunc(today()),date9.));

%let in = C:\\file\\Data;   * Jut change the file path accordingly;*

%let out = C:\\file\\Data;

%let file =Report.xlsx;

%let outfile = NewReport.xlsx;


proc import datafile="&in\&file"

        out = dataset dbms=xlsx replace;

      sheet = 'Report_name;
run;
```

5.2 Create a new file

```
OPTIONS FORMCHAR="|----|+|---+=|-/\<>*";

ods noresults;

ods excel file="&out\\&outfile"

options(sheet_name="Test_Source_Data" embedded_titles="no" start_at="1,1");

proc print data=well;run;

ods excel close;
```

5.3 Using tagset.tableeditor

```
ods tagsets.tableeditor file="&out\pivot_table.js"

   options(update_target="&out\\&outfile"

      output_type="script"

      sheet_name="Test_Source_Data"

            pivot_sheet_name="Report_summary"

            pivotpage="sex"

      pivotrow="Name"

            pivotcol="Visit"

            pivotdata="Visit"
```

```
*Continued in the same ODS  block;
Options:

          /* If it is for categorical data using 'cnt':


                    pivotdata_stats= 'Cnt'


          /* if for numeric data such as paid amount using 'sum':

                    pivotdata_stats= 'sum'

                    pivotdata_fmt="8."

     /*if for dollor amount:*/


                    /*  pivotdata_fmt="$#,###.##" */



     /* Multiple variables can be put in the pivot table:


                    pivotrow="JOBTITLE,PROVIDER"

                    pivotdata="LABCOUNT,NOTKPHC"

                    pivotdata_caption="Lab Tests1, Lab Tests 2"

                    pivotdata_stats="sum,sum"

                    PIVOTDATA_TOCOLUMNS="yes"

                    pivot_format="medium9"
                                                        */
```

*/*Continued in the same ODS block:*/*

```
        pivot_format="light9"

        pivot_grandtotal="Yes"

        pivot_subtotal="yes"

    /*Other options:

            Pivot_title="&report_name"

            excel_save_prompt="NO"

        excel_save_dialog="NO"

            open_excel="no"   */


        excel_save_file="&out\\&outfile"

        quit="Yes");
data _null_;

file print;
put _all_;
run;

ods tagsets.tableeditor   close;

/* A  Java script codes has been created in the out folder */
```

5.4 Call the Javascript file to run and a pivot table is created in the new excel file

```
x "'&out\pivot_table.js'";
```

5.5 Output of the pivot table

sex	(All)	▼	
Count of Visit	**Column Labels** ▼		
Row Labels ▼		Yes	Grand Total
A	495	67	562
B	1430		1430
C	407	173	580
D	132		132
E	420		420
F	524		524
G	2029		2029
H	965	144	1109
I	508		508
Grand Total	**6910**	**384**	**7294**

6. Export json file

A **JSON** file is a file that stores simple data structures and objects in JavaScript Object Notation (JSON) format, which is a standard data interchange format. It is primarily used for transmitting data between a web application and a server. We can easily create a json file using the proc json statement.

```
/*********************************************************************************

/* Use the JSON procedure to add output in JSON representation.  */
/* The PRETTY option makes the output easy to view.              */
/*********************************************************************************


proc json out="C:\test\testfile" pretty;
   export sashelp.cars(where=(type="SUV" and origin="USA" and drivetrain="All"
       and cylinders=4));
run;
```

If you want to view the data, you can also open with UltraEdit.

```
{
  "SASJSONExport": "1.0 PRETTY",
  "SASTableData+CARS": [
    {
      "Make": "Jeep",
      "Model": " Liberty Sport",
      "Type": "SUV",
      "Origin": "USA",
      "DriveTrain": "All",
      "MSRP": 20130,
      "Invoice": 18973,
      "EngineSize": 2.4,
      "Cylinders": 4,
      "Horsepower": 150,
      "MPG_City": 20,
      "MPG_Highway": 24,
      "Weight": 3826,
      "Wheelbase": 104,
      "Length": 174
    },
```

```json
{
    "Make": "Saturn",
    "Model": " VUE",
    "Type": "SUV",
    "Origin": "USA",
    "DriveTrain": "All",
    "MSRP": 20585,
    "Invoice": 19238,
    "EngineSize": 2.2,
    "Cylinders": 4,
    "Horsepower": 143,
    "MPG_City": 21,
    "MPG_Highway": 26,
    "Weight": 3381,
    "Wheelbase": 107,
    "Length": 181
  }
]
}
```

Chapter 5

Macro

SAS macro variables can help to make your program more compact and avoid having to type repeated codes since macros allow you to substitute text in a program and to do many other things. You should already have noticed some macro variables used in Chapter 4, which involves an ampersand (&) and percentage sign (%).

1. Macro variable

A macro variable can be assigned a value with a **%LET** statement. The expression to the right of the equal sign is the value assigned to the macro variable.

We retrieve the value by using an ampersand (&) in front of the macro variable.

```
%let list =  Apple Beer Candy;
%put  &list ;
```

From the **LOG** tab, you can see the phrase 'Apple Beer Candy'.

```
    CODE        LOG       RESULTS

 ▸ Errors, Warnings, Notes


1               OPTIONS NONOTES NOSTIMER NOSOURCE NOSYNTAXCHECK;
70
71              %let list =  Apple Beer Candy;
72
73              %put  &list ;
Apple Beer Candy
74
75
76              OPTIONS NONOTES NOSTIMER NOSOURCE NOSYNTAXCHECK;
87
```

2. Create a macro program

You can invoke a macro any number of times in a single program.

Each macro you define has a distinct name, which is subject to the standard SAS naming conventions. A macro program is defined between a **%MACRO** statement and a **%MEND** (macro end) statement, as follows:

%MACRO
macro-name;
macro definition
%MEND
macro-name;

2.1 Create a data set score then print the sub data sets

```
data score;
  input  id gender race class section
       English Math Biology History Chemistry;
datalines;
270 0 4 1 1 57 52 41 47 57
131 1 4 2 3 68 59 53 63 61
186 0 4 3 1 44 33 54 58 31
134 0 4 3 3 63 44 47 53 56
162 0 4 2 2 47 52 57 53 61
145 1 4 2 2 44 52 51 63 61
150 0 3 2 1 50 59 42 53 61
211 0 1 2 2 34 46 45 39 36
184 0 4 2 1 63 57 54 51 63
248 1 3 2 2 57 55 52 50 51
375 1 4 2 3 60 46 51 53 61
460 1 4 2 2 57 65 51 63 61
195 0 4 3 2 73 60 71 61 71
106 0 4 3 2 54 63 57 55 46
238 0 3 1 2 45 57 50 31 56
;
run;
```

2.1 Create three subsets using the output statement

```
data set1 set2 set3;
set score;
if 0 <= id <= 150 then output set1;
if 201 <= id <= 300 then output set2;
if id >= 301 then output set3;
run;
```

2.2 Print all three subsets using macro

```
%macro print;
    %do i = 1 %to 3;
    proc print data = set&i;
    run;
    %end;
%mend;

%print;
```

Obs	id	gender	race	class	section	English	Math	Biology	History	Chemistry
1	131	1	4	2	3	68	59	53	63	61
2	131	0	4	3	3	63	44	47	53	56
3	145	1	4	2	2	44	52	51	63	61
4	150	0	3	2	1	50	59	42	53	61
5	106	0	4	3	2	54	63	57	55	46
6	116	0	4	1	1	42	49	43	50	56

Obs	id	gender	race	class	section	English	Math	Biology	History	Chemistry
1	270	0	4	1	1	57	52	41	47	57
2	211	0	1	2	2	34	46	45	39	36
3	248	1	3	2	2	57	55	52	50	51
4	238	0	3	1	2	45	57	50	31	56
5	295	0	4	2	1	57	57	60	56	52

Obs	id	gender	race	class	section	English	Math	Biology	History	Chemistry
1	375	1	4	2	3	60	46	51	53	61
2	460	1	4	2	2	57	65	51	63	61
3	376	0	4	3	2	47	52	51	50	56

2.3 Combine the subset using macro

```
%macro combine;
 data all;
  set
  %do i = 1 %to 3;
    set&i
  %end;
%mend;

%combine;
```

The macro is equivalent to the following codes. If you have many datasets, like over 10, using macro will be more efficient.

```
data all;
set set1
   set2
   set3;
run;
```

2.4 Pass variable in macro program

```
%macro print_mean(num);
   %do i = 1 %to &num;
      proc print data = set&i;
      run;

      proc means data = set&i;
      var English Math Biology History Chemistry;
      run;
   %end;
%mend;
%print_mean(3);
```

The macro program has a great advantage if you have many subsets , like 15 for example. What you need to do is to change num from 3 to 15.

```
%print_mean(15);
```

3. System Macro

SAS has many system-defined macro variables. You can use the %put statement again to display the values of these system-defined macro variables. You can find more examples of system macro in Chapter 8 and Chapter 11.

%put _automatic_;

The most commonly used system macros are :
SYSDATE
SYSDATE9
SYSDAY

%put &SYSDATE9;

4. Create macro list using proc sql

If you have followed through from chapter 2, you should have created a data set named 'Inventory' . You can use the INTO clause to create a macro variable 'MakerList' with a list of the 4 car models.

If the INTO statement results in multiple values then the 'separated by' option can be used to separate those values into a desired format.

The following is the SAS codes you can use to create a car maker list from the dataset 'Inventory'.

```
LIBNAME mydata '/home/ver/project/TEMP';

proc sql;
```

```
select distinct maker into: MakerList separated by ','
from mydata.Inventory;
quit;
```

4.1 Use proc print to show the data and use %put to reveal the value of macro variable

```
proc print data = mydata.Inventory;
run;
```

Obs	maker	model	mpg	weight	price
1	AM	CON	22	2930	4090
2	AC	PAC	17	3350	4849
3	AB	SPI	22	2645	3699
4	BK	CRY	20	3250	4836
5	BN	ELA	16	4089	7825

```
%put  &MakerList;
```

Highlight the above codes and hit the run icon. You can see the value of &MakerList from the **LOG** tab.

5. Call existing SAS program

We can use **%include** to call the existing SAS program to reuse the SAS codes.

Here is the example to call a SAS program called 'Total_Expense.sas'.

```
%include "C:\home\Total_Expense.sas";
```

This is very helpful especially if you have worked on complicated projects.

Chapter 6

Array

When we have repetitive data, it is most efficient to use a SAS array to minimize the coding. SAS arrays are another way to temporarily group and refer to SAS variables. A SAS array is not a new data structure, the array name is not a variable, and arrays do not define additional variables. Rather, a SAS array provides a different name to reference a group of variables.

An array and a loop can make good use of multiple arrays which may allow us to simplify big data processing. We can use arrays to help read and analyze repetitive data with a minimum of coding. Arrays and loops can make the program much smaller and compact.

Once the array has been defined, the programmer is now able to perform the same tasks for a series of related variables, the array elements.

The **ARRAY statement** :

array array-name {n} <$>

The ARRAY statements provides the following information about the SAS array:
- array-name – Any valid SAS name
- n – Number of elements within the array
- $ - Indicates the elements within the array are character type variables
- length – A common length for the array elements
- elements – List of SAS variables to be part of the array

Tip: The default type of array elements is numeric. Using $ only when the array elements are character.

1. Create new data set using array

Let's create a data set with 5 items;

```
data cost;
  input OrderID item1-item5;
datalines;

1 128 341 311 200 170
2 484 308 310 315 800
3 601 612 613 619 150
;
run;
```

Obs	OrderID	item1	item2	item3	item4	item5
1	1	128	341	311	200	170
2	2	484	308	310	315	800
3	3	601	612	613	619	150

We can use an array to add new 50% discount variables for each item and set those less than 200 to zero.

```
data discount;
set cost;
  array item(5) item1-item5;
  array discount(5) discount1-discount5;
  array cut(5) cut1- cut5;

  do i = 1 to 5;
    discount[i] =item[i]*0.5 ;        /* Get 50% discount*/
     cut[i] = discount[i];            /* set new variables to discount values*/
     if  item[i] <200 then cut[i] =0;  /* if discount<200, set the new value to zero*/
  end;

     sum = sum(of discount:);          /* Get sum variable */
      if sum >800 then output = 'Yes';

  drop i;
run;

proc print data = discount;  run;
```

Obs	OrderID	item1	item2	item3	item4	item5	item6	item7	item8	item9	item10	discount1	discount2	discount3	discount4	discount5	cut1	cut2	cut3	cut4	cut5
1	1	128	341	311	200	170	350	311	319	351	234	64.0	170.5	155.5	100.0	85	0.0	170.5	155.5	100.0	0
2	2	484	308	310	315	800	600	153	214	381	324	242.0	154.0	155.0	157.5	400	242.0	154.0	155.0	157.5	400
3	3	601	612	613	619	150	620	618	632	312	202	300.5	306.0	306.5	309.5	75	300.5	306.0	306.5	309.5	0

2. Restructure data set using array

2.1 Reshaping wide to long

*Original dataset;

```
data cost;
  input OrderID item1-item10 ;
datalines;
1 128 341 311 200 170 350 311 319 351 234 813
2 484 308 310 315 800 600 153 214 381 324 471
3 601 612 613 619 150 620 618 632 312 202 215
;
run;
```

Obs	OrderID	item1	item2	item3	item4	item5	item6	item7	item8	item9	item10
1	1	128	341	311	200	170	350	311	319	351	234
2	2	484	308	310	315	800	600	153	214	381	324
3	3	601	612	613	619	150	620	618	632	312	202

* Create a dataset from wide to long;

```
data cost_long;
set cost;
 array st[10] item1 - item10;
 do item = 1 to 10;
   cost = st[item];
   output;
 end;
  drop item1 - item10;
run;

proc print data=cost_long;
run;
```

Obs	OrderID	item	cost
1	1	1	128
2	1	2	341
3	1	3	311
4	1	4	200
5	1	5	170
6	1	6	350
7	1	7	311
8	1	8	319
9	1	9	351
10	1	10	234
11	2	1	484
12	2	2	308
13	2	3	310
14	2	4	315
15	2	5	800
16	2	6	600
17	2	7	153
18	2	8	214
19	2	9	381
20	2	10	324
21	3	1	601
22	3	2	612

63

23	3	3	613
24	3	4	619
25	3	5	150
26	3	6	620
27	3	7	618
28	3	8	632
29	3	9	312
30	3	10	202

There is an alternative way to do the same thing by using **proc transpose** .

```
proc transpose data = cost out = cost1 (rename=(col1=cost ))name=product  label=cost;
by OrderID;
var item1 - item10;
run;
proc print data = cost1;
run;
```

Obs	OrderID	product	cost
1	1	item1	128
2	1	item2	341
3	1	item3	311
4	1	item4	200
5	1	item5	170
6	1	item6	350
7	1	item7	311
8	1	item8	319
9	1	item9	351
10	1	item10	234
11	2	item1	484
12	2	item2	308
13	2	item3	310
14	2	item4	315
15	2	item5	800
16	2	item6	600
17	2	item7	153
18	2	item8	214
19	2	item9	381
20	2	item10	324
21	3	item1	601

22	3	item2	612
23	3	item3	613
24	3	item4	619
25	3	item5	150
26	3	item6	620
27	3	item7	618
28	3	item8	632
29	3	item9	312
30	3	item10	202

2.2 Reshaping long to wide

In order to reshape the dataset from long to wide, **FIRST**, **LAST** and **RETAIN** statements will be used. The long data set , cost_long which was created in 6.2.1 is used here to get started.

```
proc sort data = cost_long;
by OrderID item;
run;

data wide_array;
  set cost_long;
  by OrderID;

  retain item1 - item10;
  array Af(10) item1 – item10;

  if first.OrderID then do;
    do i = 1 to 10;
      Af[i] = .;
    end;                        /*Initialize array */
  end;

  Af(item) = cost;             /*looping across values in the variable year*/
  if last.OrderID then output;  /* outputs only the last obs in a family*/

  drop year faminc i;

run;
```

```
proc print data=wide_array;
run;
```

Obs	OrderID	item	cost	item1	item2	item3	item4	item5	item6	item7	item8	item9	item10
1	1	10	234	128	341	311	200	170	350	311	319	351	234
2	2	10	324	484	308	310	315	800	600	153	214	381	324
3	3	10	202	601	612	613	619	150	620	618	632	312	202

3. Use multidimensional array

Let's say we have a data set with multiple observations or multiple rows per subject, which is called **weight**. Then, we can use a two dimensional array to create a new dataset with one observation or one line per subject.

* Create a new data set ;

```
data weight;
  input ID level time weight ;
datalines;
01 1 1 165
01 1 2 159
01 1 3 154
01 2 1 213
01 2 2 197
02 1 1 112
02 1 2 113
02 1 3 127
02 2 1 245
02 2 2 234
02 2 3 230
;
run;

proc print data = weight;
run;
```

The following is what the data looks like in the SAS output session.

Obs	ID	level	time	weight
1	1	1	1	165
2	1	1	2	159
3	1	1	3	154
4	1	2	1	213
5	1	2	2	197
6	2	1	1	112
7	2	1	2	113
8	2	1	3	127
9	2	2	1	245
10	2	2	2	234
11	2	2	3	230

The data weight contains information for two subject ID = 1 and ID =2, with 3 levels and 3 times. A two dimensional array(2,3) can be used to represent the weight at different **level** and **time**.

```
proc sort data = weight;
by ID level time;
run;

data weight_perID;
array wt[2,3] wt1 - wt6;
retain wt1 -wt6;
set weight;
by ID;

if first.ID then
 do i = 1 to 2;
   do j = 1 to 3;
     wt[i,j] =.;
   end;
 end;

wt[level,time] = weight;

if last.ID then output;
keep ID wt1 -wt6;
run;
```

67

```
proc print data = weight_perID;
run;
```

Obs	wt1	wt2	wt3	wt4	wt5	wt6	ID
1	165	159	154	213	197	198	1
2	112	113	127	245	234	230	2

Tips: Proc transpose only works for one dimension, only one ID per transpose limitation.

The general syntax of **proc transpose** is:

```
PROC TRANSPOSE DATA=D1 OUT=D2 NAME = column that was transfered
              PREFIX = The desired column name ;
    BY variable(s);
    ID variable;
    VAR variable(s);
RUN;
```

PREFIX option provides a prefix value of transposed column names instead of col1, col2, col3, col4, col5, col6 etc.

NAME option provides the name for an output file column which tells which input variables were transposed.

BY statement names the row identification variable. It requires a preliminary PROC SORT.

ID statement names the columns in the input file whose row values provide the column names in the output file. There only should be one variable in the ID statement.

If the ID values are numeric which can't be used as SAS column name, so use the PREFIX option with the ID statement to create variables like 'Item100', 'item200'.

For this example, ID values are 100, 200, 300..., we set prefix = Item. The column name of the transposed file becomes 'Item100', 'Item200', 'Item300'.

VAR statement specifies the variables which will be transposed. The variable value can be character or numeric.

68

Chapter 7

System time

When we set up the automation process using SAS, getting the system time becomes very common practice. The previous week, previous month, quarter or year are some of the frequently used system time in SAS programming.

We have to output different date formats for different files. In this section, we display all popular data formats in SAS coding. Here are the examples:

1. The begin and end date of previous week

```
Data _null_;

call
symputx('week_begin',put(intnx('week',today(),-1,'b'),date9.));

call
symputx('week_end',put(intnx('week',today(),-1,'e'),date9.));

run;

%put &week_begin   &week_end;
```

2 .The first date of previous month and previous year

```
Data _null_;

call symputx('week1',put(intnx('week',today(),-1,'b'),date9.));

call symputx('week2',put(intnx('week',today(),-1,'e'),date9.));

call
symputx('pre_month',put(intnx('month',today(),-1,'b'),date9.));

call
symputx('yearmonth',put(intnx('month',today(),-1,'b'),yymmn6.));

call symputx('year1',put(intnx('year',today(),-0,'b'),date9.));
run;

%put  &yearmonth &pre_month &year1;
```

3. The first date of previous quarter

```
Data _null_;

call
symputx('begin',put(intnx('quarter',today(),-1,'b'),date9.));

call symputx('end',put(intnx('quarter',today(),-1,'e'),date9.));

call symputx('qtr',put(intnx('quarter',today(),-1,'b'),qtr4.));

call symputx('year',put(intnx('quarter',today(),-1,'b'),year4.));

run;

%put &begin  &end   &qtr    &year;
```

4. The begin and last date of previous month

```sas
Data _null_;

 call
symputx('Prev_month_begin_dt',put(intnx('month',today(),-1,'b'),date9.));

 call
symputx('Prev_month_end_dt',put(intnx('month',today(),-1,'e'),date9.));

 call
symputx('report_year',substr(put(intnx('month',today(),-1,'e'),yymmddn8.)
,1,4));

 call symputx('yearmonth',put(intnx('month',today(),-1,'b'),yymmn6.));

run;


%put &Prev_month_begin_dt &Prev_month_end_dt  &report_year

&yearmonth;
```

5. The begin and last date of previous quarter

```
%let dt=%sysfunc(date());

%let beg=%sysfunc(putn(%sysfunc(intnx(quarter,&dt, -1,
begin)),date9.));

%let end=%sysfunc(putn(%sysfunc(intnx(quarter,&dt, -1,
end)),date9.));

%let rd=%sysfunc(putn(%sysfunc(date()),yymmddn8.));

%let dtt=%sysfunc(putn(%sysfunc(today()),yymmddn8.));

%let dtt1=%sysfunc(putn(%sysfunc(today()),date9.));

%put  &beg &end  &rd &dtt &dtt1;
```

6. The begin and last date of previous year

```
%let dt = %sysfunc(date());

%let beg = %sysfunc(putn(%sysfunc(intnx(month,&dt, -1,
begin)),date9.));

%let end = %sysfunc(putn(%sysfunc(intnx(month,&dt, -1, end)),date9.));

%let rd = %sysfunc(putn(%sysfunc(date()),yymmddn8.));

%put &dt &rd &beg &end;
```

7. The current year and date

```
%let yr =

%sysfunc(putn(%sysfunc(intnx(year,%sysfunc(date())),0)),year4.));

%let dt =
%sysfunc(putn(%sysfunc(intnx(day,%sysfunc(today())),-0)),date9.));

%put &dt &yr;
```

7.1 The current year month

```
%let monthyear = %sysfunc(putn(%sysfunc(date()),yymmn6.));

%put &monthyear;
```

7.2 The year month which is 10 months after a specific date (01JAN2017)

```
%let month =

%sysfunc(substrn(%sysfunc(putn(%sysfunc(intnx(month, '01JAN2017'D,10)),da
te9.)),3));

%put &month;
```

NOV2017

```
*The current year, month, and date;

%let rd = %sysfunc(putn(%sysfunc(date()),yymmddn8.));

%put &rd;
```

8. The previous year and month

```
%let dt =%sysfunc(date(), date9.);

%put &dt;




%let yearmonth1 =  %sysfunc(putn(%sysfunc(intnx(month,"&dt"d, -1,
begin)),yymmddn8.));

%let yearmonth2 =  %sysfunc(putn(%sysfunc(intnx(month,"&dt"d, -1,
begin)),yymmn6.));

%put &yearmonth1  &yearmonth2;



  *Method2;

%let monthyear1  =
%sysfunc(PUTN(%eval(%sysfunc(date())-1),monyy7.));

%let monthyear2  =
%sysfunc(PUTN(%eval(%sysfunc(date())-1),yymmn6.));

%put &monthyear1 &monthyear2;
```

8.1 The previous month for a specified date

```
%let cmon =
%sysfunc(putn(%sysfunc(intnx(month,%sysfunc(date())),-1)),yymmn6.));

%put &cmon;


%let
Month =
%sysfunc(substrn(%sysfunc(putn(%sysfunc(intnx(month,'01JAN2017'd,10)),dat
e9.)),3));

%put &month;
```

NOV2017

```
*The variation format of  the beginning of previous month;

Data _null_;

call symputx('yearmont',put(intnx('month',today(),-1,'b'),date9.));

call symputx('yearmonth1',put(intnx('month',today(),-1,'b'),yymmddn8.));

call symputx('yearmonth2',put(intnx('month',today(),-1,'b'),yymmn6.));

call
symputx('ymh',substr(put(intnx('month',today(),-1,'e'),yymmddn8.),1,6));

run;

%put &yearmont  &yearmonth1  &yearmonth2 &ymh;
```

8.2 The first day of the month (24 months prior today)

```
Data _null_;

call symputx('yearmont',put(intnx('month',today(),-24,'b'),date9.));


call symputx('yearmonth',put(intnx('month',today(),-24,'b'),yymmn6.));


call
symputx('yearmonth1',put(intnx('month',today(),-24,'b'),mmddyy10.));

call symputx('month',put(intnx('month',today(),-24,'b'),date9.));


call
symputx('report_year',substr(put(intnx('month',today(),-24,'e'),yymmdd
n8.),1,4));


call
symputx('report_yearmonth',substr(put(intnx('month',today(),-24,'b'),d
ate9.),3,7));
run;

%put &yearmont  &yearmonth &yearmonth1 &report_year &report_yearmonth;
```

8.3 The variety format for the first day of the month (24 months prior today)

```
Data _null_;

call
symputx('yearmonth1',put(intnx('month',today(),-24,'b'),mmddyy10.));

call
symputx('yearmonth2',put(intnx('month',today(),-24,'b'),yymmdd8.));

call
symputx('yearmonth3',put(intnx('month',today(),-24,'b'),yymmdd10.));

call
symputx('yearmonth4',put(intnx('month',today(),-24,'b'),yymmdd10.));

call
symputx('yearmonth5',put(intnx('month',today(),-24,'b'),yymmdds8.));

call
symputx('yearmonth6',put(intnx('month',today(),-24,'b'),yymmddn8.));

call
symputx('YearMonthDate',put(intnx('month',today(),-24,'b'),date9.));

;

run;

%put &yearmonth1 &yearmonth2 &yearmonth3 &yearmonth4 &yearmonth5
&yearmonth6;


%put &yearmonth6  &YearMonthDate   &YearMonthDate


/* Similarly, You can replace month with week to get relevant date for prior week*/
```

8.4 If a day is Monday (&num Equals 2), get last Friday

```
%macro weekday;

%let  num=%sysfunc(weekday(%sysfunc(today())));

%put  &num;

%if %sysfunc(weekday(%sysfunc(today())))=2 %then  %do;

%let uu = %sysfunc(PUTN(%eval(%sysfunc(date())-3),date9.));

%put &uu;

%let aa = %sysfunc(PUTN(%eval(%sysfunc(date())-3),yymmddn8.));

%put &aa;

%end;

%mend ;

%weekday ;
```

8.5 Get previous Wednesday

```
%let date =%eval(%sysfunc(today())-1);
%put &date;
%Let wk=%sysfunc(putn(
%sysfunc(intnx(week.4,&date,0,beginning)),date9.));
%put &wk;
```

Chapter 8
Format and Label

FORMAT and LABEL statements are assigning temporary or permanent attributes to data variables. Some procedures use labels automatically. It's very common practice to use user defined labels.

1. Assigns descriptive labels to variables

The syntax is ;

LABEL *variable-1* =*'label-1'*;

Let's start to work on the original data set and add labels to variable item1 to item4 using data step and proc sql.

1.1 Add label using data step

Obs	OrderID	item1	item2	item3	item4
1	1	128	341	311	200
2	2	484	308	310	315
3	3	601	612	613	619

```
data label_set;

set label_set;

label item1 = 'Computer monitor'

    item2 = 'Projector'

    item3 = 'TV'

    item4 = 'foot massager';

run;
```

proc print data = label_set label;run;

Obs	OrderID	Computer monitor	Projector	TV	Foot massager
1	1	128	341	311	200
2	2	484	308	310	315
3	3	601	612	613	619

1.2 Add label using proc sql

```
proc sql;

create table label_set as

select OrderID, item1 label =  'Computer monitor',

item2 label = 'Projector', item3 label = 'TV',

item4 label = 'Foot massager'

from label_set;

quit;
```

2. Assign value labels to variables using format

There are two types of formats in SAS, system format and user defined format. System formats are built in format such as date format (date9.) and date time format(datetime25.), you can't change the system format.

You will have to create a user defined format to get your data more readable.

2.1 Create user defined format using proc format

The syntax of defining a format is :

```
PROC FORMAT;
   VALUE format-name

     Data-value-1 = 'Label 1'
     Data-value-2 = 'Label 2';

   VALUE format-name-2

     Data-value-3 = 'Label 3'
     Data-value-4 = 'Label 4';
     .....;
RUN;
```

Remember to use a dot after the format name when using a format.

Let's see the example. The following is the original dataset.

Obs	CaseNumber	Gender	Age
1	1	1	57
2	2	1	64
3	3	2	64
4	4	2	57
5	5	2	47

We create the format using the following codes.

```
proc format ;
value gender
    1 = "Female"
    2 = "Male";
run;

data format_set1;
set format_set;
format Gender $gender.;
run;
proc print data = format_set1;
run;
proc sql;
create table format_set as
select CaseNumber,  Gender format = gender.   ,  Age
from  format_set;
quit;
```

Obs	CaseNumber	Gender	Age
1	1	Female	57
2	2	Female	64
3	3	Male	64
4	4	Male	57
5	5	Male	47

3. Date formatting

There are a large variety of date formats in SAS, DATE, DATE TIME and other formats. We have covered a lot of details in Chapter 7. Let's follow through more examples here.

3.1 The variation format of the beginning of current month

```
Data _null_;
call symputx('yearmont',put(intnx('month',today(),-1,'b'),date9.));
call symputx('yearmonth1',put(intnx('month',today(),-1,'b'),yymmddn8.));
call symputx('yearmonth2',put(intnx('month',today(),-1,'b'),yymmn6.));
call symputx('ymh',substr(put(intnx('month',today(),-1,'e'),yymmddn8.),1,6));
run;
%put &yearmont &yearmonth1 &yearmonth2 &ymh;
```

3.2 Current date time in datetime format

```
data _null_;
x = today();
format x ddmmyy10.;
y = datetime();
format y datetime20.;
put "Formatted day: " x " , formatted datetime: " y;
run;
```

3.3 Different date formats

```
Data _null_;

call symputx('yearmont',put(intnx('month',today(),-24,'b'),date9.));

call symputx('yearmonth',put(intnx('month',today(),-24,'b'),yymmn6.));

call symputx('yearmonth1',put(intnx('month',today(),-24,'b'),mmddyy10.));

call symputx('month',put(intnx('month',today(),-24,'b'),date9.));

call symputx('report_year',substr(put(intnx('month',today(),-24,'e'),yymmddn8.),1,4));

call symputx('report_yearmonth',substr(put(intnx('month',today(),-24,'b'),date9.),3,7));
run;

%put &yearmont &yearmonth &yearmonth1 &report_year &report_yearmonth;
```

```
01JUN2017   201706  06/01/2017  2017  JUN2017
```

```
Data _null_;

call symputx('date1',put(intnx('month',today(),-1,'b'),mmddyy10.));

call symputx('date2',put(intnx('month',today(),-1,'b'),yymmdd8.));

call symputx('date3',put(intnx('month',today(),-1,'b'),yymmdd10.));

call symputx('date4',put(intnx('month',today(),-1,'b'),yymmdd10.));

call symputx('date5',put(intnx('month',today(),-1,'b'),yymmdds8.));

call symputx('date6',put(intnx('month',today(),-1,'b'),yymmddn8.));

run;
```

%put &date1 &date2 &date3 &date4 &date5 &date6 ;

```
06/01/2019  19-06-01  2019-06-01  2019-06-01  19/06/01  20190601
```

3.4 Get the specific date

We need to get one specific date for automation using weekday() function which produces an integer that represents the day of the week, where 1=Sunday, 2=Monday, . . . , 7=Saturday.. In this example, we alway get Friday. We check if a day is Monday (&num Equals 2), then we get the last Friday.

```
%macro weekday;
%let  num=%sysfunc(weekday(%sysfunc(today())));
%put  &num;
%if %sysfunc(weekday(%sysfunc(today())))=2 %then  %do;
%let uu = %sysfunc(PUTN(%eval(%sysfunc(date())-3),date9.));
%put &uu;
%let aa = %sysfunc(PUTN(%eval(%sysfunc(date())-3),yymmddn8.));
%put &aa;
%end;
%mend ;

%weekday ;
```

3.5 User defined format

We will create a user defined format (**mdyhms**) to Convert DATETIME20. to MM/DD/YYYY HH:MM:SS

```
proc format;
picture mdyhms other = '%0m/%0d/%Y %0H:%0M:%0S' (datatype=datetime);
run;
data date1;
input date $50.;
cards;
28-05-2011:10:21:20
27-05-2012:14:22:26
27-05-2013:11:36:33
27-05-2014:17:14:55
;
run;

proc print data = date1;
run;
```

```
data date2;

set date1;

TransformedDate=input(date,anydtdtm.);

format TransformedDate mdyhms. ;

run;

proc print data = date2;

run;
```

date	TransformedDate
28-05-2011:10:21:20	05/28/2011 10:21:20
27-05-2012:14:22:26	05/27/2012 14:22:26
27-05-2013:11:36:33	05/27/2013 11:36:33
27-05-2014:17:14:55	05/27/2014 17:14:55

4. Convert character input to datetime

In reality, we will encounter time date data as character so we will have to convert the character data to datetime data in different formats.

4.1 Convert from YYYY-MM-DD to DD/MM/YYYY

```
data testdate;

    length chardate $10;

    infile datalines;

    input chardate $;

    date = input(chardate,yymmdd10.);

    date1 = input(chardate,yymmdd10.);

    Format date date9. date1 mmddyy10.;

datalines;

2011-01-01
1960-01-01
1984-11-29
2013-03-29
;
run;

proc print data = testdate;
run;
```

chardate	date	date1
2011-01-01	01JAN2011	01/01/2011
1960-01-01	01JAN1960	01/01/1960
1984-11-29	29NOV1984	11/29/1984
2013-03-29	29MAR2013	03/29/2013

4.2 Convert from DDMONYYYY to DD/MM/YYYY

```
data testdate2;

    length chardate $10;

    infile datalines;

    input chardate $;

    date = input(chardate,DATE9.);

    date1 = input(chardate,DATE9.);

    FORMAT date yymmdd10. date1 mmddyy10.;

return;

datalines;

10SEP2019
09SEP2019
03SEP2019
19SEP2019
;
run;

proc print data = testdate2;
run;
```

chardate	date	date1
10SEP2019	2019-09-10	09/10/2019
09SEP2019	2019-09-09	09/09/2019
03SEP2019	2019-09-03	09/03/2019
19SEP2019	2019-09-19	09/19/2019

4.4 Convert from DD-MON-YYYY to DATETIME

```
data date_formats;

input date $50.;

cards;

28-MAY-2014:10:21:20
27-MAY-2014:14:22:26
27-MAY-2014:11:36:33
27-MAY-2014:17:14:55
;
run;


data out;

set date_formats;

new_date=input(date,anydtdtm.); /*converting character to date format */

format new_date datetime18.;    /* Printing the data into wanted format */
run;

proc print data = out;

run;
```

date	new_date
28-MAY-2014:10:21:20	28MAY14:10:21:02
27-MAY-2014:14:22:26	27MAY14:14:22:02
27-MAY-2014:11:36:33	27MAY14:11:36:03
27-MAY-2014:17:14:55	27MAY14:17:14:05

4.5 Convert yyyymmdd(numeric) to DATE9 format

```
data test;

input date ;

format date1 date9. date2 yymmdd10. date3 mmddyy10. ;

date1 = input(put(date,8.),yymmdd8.);

date2 = input(put(date,8.),yymmdd10.);

date3 = date1;

cards;

20161201
20150610
20171203

run;


proc print;

run;
```

date	date1	date2	date3
20161201	01DEC2016	2016-12-01	12/01/2016
20150610	10JUN2015	2015-06-10	06/10/2015
20171203	03DEC2017	2017-12-03	12/03/2017

4.6 Format date as the quarter of the year in the form of Q1, Q2, Q3, Q4 and the month of the year

```
data test1;

informat date mmddyy10.;
format date mmddyy10.;
input date;
cards;

01/31/2012
04/05/2015
09/09/2016
12/02/2017
;
run;

data test2;

set test1;

date1 = put(date,mmddyyn.);

data2 = put(date,date9.);

data3 = put(date,yymmdd10.);

*YYQtr;

YYQtr = put(date,yyq4.);

*YYYYQtr;

YYYYQtr = put(date,yyq6.);

*YYMM;

YYMonth = put(date,yymmn6.);

run;

proc print;run;
```

date	date1	data2	data3	YYQtr	YYYYQtr	YYMM
01/31/2012	01312012	31JAN2012	2012-01-31	12Q1	2012Q1	201201
04/05/2015	04052015	05APR2015	2015-04-05	15Q2	2015Q2	201504
09/09/2016	09092016	09SEP2016	2016-09-09	16Q3	2016Q3	201609
12/02/2017	12022017	02DEC2017	2017-12-02	17Q4	2017Q4	201712

Tips:

- PUT() always creates character variables.
- INPUT() can create character or numeric variables based on the informat.
- The source format must match the source variable type in PUT().
- The source variable type for INPUT() must always be character variables.

Chapter 9

Data manipulation

We have created many data sets in Chapter 4. Data step and proc sql are the two major ways to manipulate the data sets.

1. Data set sub setting

Let's look at the data Inventory:

Obs	maker	model	mpg	weight	price
1	AM	CON	22	2930	4090
2	AC	PAC	17	3350	4849
3	AB	SPI	22	2645	3699
4	BK	CRY	20	3250	4836
5	BN	ELA	16	4089	7825

1.1 Use IF statement and Logical operators (=,<, >, or, in)

```
data inventory1;
set inventory;
if mpg >= 20 and Maker in ('AB','BK');
run;
```

Obs	maker	model	mpg	weight	price
1	AB	SPI	22	2645	3699
2	BK	CRY	20	3250	4836

1.2 Use where statement and Logical operators (=,<, >, or, in)

```
data inventory2;
set inventory;
where mpg >= 20 and Maker in ('AB','BK');
run;
```

Tip: Using **IF** and **WHERE** statements will produce the same data set but Where statement will be more efficient than IF statement especially for large datasets.

1.3 Use proc sql

```
proc sql;
create table inventory1  as
select * from inventory
where mpg >= 20 and Maker in ('AB','BK');
quit;
```

Data step and proc sql statement can be used to create the same data set.

2. Concatenate datasets

Combine data sets with similar structure.

There are two data sets:

```
data inventory_1;
set inventory;
where maker = 'AC';
run;
```

Obs	maker	model	mpg	weight	price
1	AC	PAC	17	3350	4849

```
data inventory_2;
set inventory;
where maker = 'BK';
run;
```

Obs	maker	model	mpg	weight	price
1	BK	CRY	20	3250	4836

2.1 Combine data sets using SET statement

```
data all;
set inventory_1 inventory_2;
run;
```

Obs	maker	model	mpg	weight	price
1	AC	PAC	17	3350	4849
2	BK	CRY	20	3250	4836

2.2 Combine datasets using PROC SQL and UNION statement

```
proc sql;
create table all as
select * from inventory
where maker = 'AC'
union
select * from inventory
where maker = 'BK';
quit;
```

The above codes generate the identical data as the date step statement.

3. Merge datasets

Combining different data sets: Balance

Obs	AccountNumber	Week1	Week4	Balance
1	2477	195	163	32
2	2431	220	198	22
3	2456	173	155	18
4	2412	135	116	19

Data set: Level

Obs	AccountNumber	Level	Year
1	2412	High	2016
2	2456	Low	2001
3	2477	High	1990

3.1 Combine data sets using merge statement

We try to combine two datasets 'Balance' and 'Level'.

First, we sought the data first by Account Number. If the data is not sorted, the error will pop up by using MERGE statement.

```
proc sort data = Balance;
by AccountNumber;
run;
proc sort data = Level;
by AccountNumber;
run;

data NewCombine;
merge Balance Level;
by AccountNumber;
run;
```

Merge by default is LEFT JOIN (If a), please refer to 3.4 for LEFT JOIN details.

The data set **NewCombine** has all variables in both data set **Balance** and **Level.** There is no record for account number 2431 in data set Level, therefore the **NewCombine** dataset will have missing values which are blank for character variables and a dot for numeric variables.

Obs	AccountNumber	Week1	Week4	Balance	Level	Year
1	2412	135	116	19	High	2016
2	2431	220	198	22		.
3	2456	173	155	18	Low	2001
4	2477	195	163	32	High	1990

3.2 Combine data sets using MERGE statement and IN option when merging only the matches

To avoid the missing values in the result we can consider keeping only the observations with matched values for the common variable. That is achieved by using the **IN** statement with **MERGE** statement.

The IN = data set option creates a temporary variable that can be used anywhere in the data step but is not added to the new data set.

```
proc sort data = balance;
by AccountNumber;
run;
proc sort data = Level;
by AccountNumber;
run;

data NewIn;
merge Balance (in = a) Level (in = b);
if a and b;
by AccountNumber;
run;
```

The **IN=** statement in both datasets and **IF** statement keep only the observations where the values from both the data sets Balance and Level match.

Obs	AccountNumber	Week1	Week4	Balance	Level	Year
1	2412	135	116	19	High	2016
2	2456	173	155	18	Low	2001
3	2477	195	163	32	High	1990

3.3 Combine data sets using PROC SQL and JOIN statement

PROC SQL is very useful and flexible. Here we use the JOIN statement to get data matched in both Balance and Level.

```
proc sql;
create table NewJoin as
select a.*, b.* from Balance a
join Level b on a.AccountNumber = b.AccountNumber;
quit;
proc print data = NewJoin;
run;
```

Obs	AccountNumber	Week1	Week4	Balance	Level	Year
1	2412	135	116	19	High	2016
2	2456	173	155	18	Low	2001
3	2477	195	163	32	High	1990

3.4 Combine data sets using PROC SQL and LEFT JOIN statement

The **LEFT JOIN** statement is to get data matched in data set *Balance*.

In our example, missing values (blank for character and a dot . for numeric missing value) will be added if not in the dataset *Level*.

```
proc sql;
create table NewLeft as
select a.*, b.* from Balance a
left join Level b on a.AccountNumber = b.AccountNumber;
quit;
proc print data = NewLeft;
run;
```

Obs	AccountNumber	Week1	Week4	Balance	Level	Year
1	2412	135	116	19	High	2016
2	2431	220	198	22		
3	2456	173	155	18	Low	2001
4	2477	195	163	32	High	1990

The **LEFT JOIN** statement is equivalent to a data step **IN** statement with **IF** condition (if a).

```
data NewLeft;
merge Balance (in = a) Level (in = b);
if a ;
by AccountNumber;
run;
```

3.5 Combine data sets using PROC SQL and RIGHT JOIN statement

In our example, the RIGHT JOIN statement is to get data matched in data set *LEVEL*.

Records will be excluded from the new data set if it is not in data set *Level*.

```
proc sql;
create table NewRight as
select a.*, b.* from Balance a
right join Level b on a.AccountNumber = b.AccountNumber;
quit;
proc print data = NewRight;
run;
```

Obs	AccountNumber	Week1	Week4	Balance	Level	Year
1	2412	135	116	19	High	2016
2	2456	173	155	18	Low	2001
3	2477	195	163	32	High	1990

The **RIGHT JOIN** statement is equivalent to the data step **IN** statement with **IF** condition (if b).

```
data New;
merge Balance (in = a) Level (in = b);
if b;
by AccountNumber;
run;
```

4. Update datasets

It is very common practice to update the dataset all the time. There are many ways to accomplish the task.

4.1 Update data using UPDATE statement

There is always a need to update the master data set with new information. Let's see the combined data set with missing value.

Obs	AccountNumber	Week1	Week4	Balance	Level	Year
1	2412	135	116	19	High	2016
2	2431	220	198	22		.
3	2456	173	155	18	Low	2001
4	2477	195	163	32	High	1990

We can update the missing data and other some information with the following data:

Obs	AccountNumber	Level	Year
1	2412	Low	2002
2	2431	High	2012

Let's see how we update data values for two cases (AccountNumber 2412, 2431) in the NewCombine dataset.

```
proc sort data = NewCombine;
by AccountNumber;
run;
proc sort data = NewLevel;
by AccountNumber;
run;

data updatedNew;
set NewCombine NewLevel;
by AccountNumber;
run;

proc print;
run;
```

Obs	AccountNumber	Week1	Week4	Balance	Level	Year
1	2412	135	116	19	Low	2002
2	2431	220	198	22	High	2012
3	2456	173	155	18	Low	2001
4	2477	195	163	32	High	1990

4.2 Update data using PROC SQL statement

```
proc sql;
update NewCombine
  set Level=
   case
   when AccountNumber = 2412 then 'High'
   when AccountNumber = 2431 then 'Low'
   else Level
   end,
   Year=
   case
   when AccountNumber = 2431 then 2003
   else Year
```

```
   end ;
quit;

proc print;
run;
```

The data set before update:

Obs	AccountNumber	Week1	Week4	Balance	Level	Year
1	2412	135	116	19	High	2016
2	2431	220	198	22		.
3	2456	173	155	18	Low	2001
4	2477	195	163	32	High	1990

The data set after update:

Obs	AccountNumber	Week1	Week4	Balance	Level	Year
1	2412	135	116	19	High	2016
2	2431	220	198	22	Low	2003
3	2456	173	155	18	Low	2001
4	2477	195	163	32	High	1990

4.3 Update data using IF statement in data step

We can update data in the data step using **IF** statements which generate the same result as using the **UPDATE** statement.

```
data NewCombine1;
set NewCombine;
if AccountNumber = 2412 then Level = 'High';
if AccountNumber = 2431 then Level ='Low';
if AccountNumber = 2431 then Year = 2003;
run;

proc print;
run;
```

Original data set:

Obs	AccountNumber	Week1	Week4	Balance	Level	Year
1	2412	135	116	19	High	2016
2	2431	220	198	22		.
3	2456	173	155	18	Low	2001
4	2477	195	163	32	High	1990

Updated data set:

Obs	AccountNumber	Week1	Week4	Balance	Level	Year
1	2412	135	116	19	High	2016
2	2431	220	198	22	Low	2003
3	2456	173	155	18	Low	2001
4	2477	195	163	32	High	1990

5. Dealing with duplicate records

It is common to have duplicates in the dataset. It will always be good practice to check duplicates and deal with it.

5.1 Identify duplicate

We can get the duplicate using proc sql with a **HAVE** statement.

The original data:

Obs	AccountNumber	Week1	Week4	Balance
1	2412	130	118	12
2	2477	195	163	32
3	2431	220	198	22
4	2412	130	118	12
5	2456	173	155	18
6	2412	135	116	19

Then, we use the following codes to update the dataset:

```
proc sql;
create table data_dup as
select * from balance
where AccountNumber in
 (select distinct AccountNumber from
  (select AccountNumber, count(*) from balance
group by AccountNumber
having count(*) >1
  )
);
quit;

proc print data = dup;
run;
```

We can see that only duplicated data has been pulled in the data set: data_dup.

Obs	AccountNumber	Week1	Week4	Balance
1	2412	130	118	12
2	2412	130	118	12
3	2412	135	116	19

5.2 Using RETAIN and LAG() function to identify duplicate

Original data set :Test

Obs	AccountNumber	Week1	Week4	Balance
1	2477	195	163	32
2	2431	123	220	-97
3	2414	130	121	9
4	2456	125	155	-30
5	2412	135	127	8
6	2412	135	127	8

```
proc sort data = test;
by AccountNumber;
run;

data test1;
set test;
retain span(1);
by AccountNUmber;
if Week1 =lag(Week1) then span+1;
if first.AccountNumber then span=1;
run;
```

Obs	AccountNumber	Week1	Week4	Balance	span
1	2412	135	127	8	1
2	2412	135	127	8	2
3	2414	130	121	9	1
4	2431	123	220	-97	1
5	2456	125	155	-30	1
6	2477	195	163	32	1

Span >1 indicates the duplicate in the data set. You exclude the duplicate using DELETE

```
data test2;
set test1;
if span >1 then delete;
run;
```

Obs	AccountNumber	Week1	Week4	Balance	span
1	2412	135	127	8	1
2	2414	130	121	9	1
3	2431	123	220	-97	1
4	2456	125	155	-30	1
5	2477	195	163	32	1

5.3 Remove duplicate

Original data:

Obs	AccountNumber	Week1	Week4	Balance
1	2412	130	118	12
2	2412	130	118	12
3	2412	135	116	19
4	2431	220	198	22
5	2456	173	155	18
6	2477	195	163	32

5.3.1 Using PROC SORT and NODUPKEY statement

By **_all_** statement will remove identical duplicates. Only one distinct record for Account 2412 has been kept in the data set.

```
proc sort data = balance out= balance1 nodupkey;
by _all_;
run;
proc print data = balance1;
run;
```

Obs	AccountNumber	Week1	Week4	Balance
1	2412	130	118	12
2	2412	135	116	19
3	2431	220	198	22
4	2456	173	155	18
5	2477	195	163	32

If we only want to keep one record for each account number, we can use a **BY** statement.

```
proc sort data = balance out= balance1 nodupkey;
by AccountNumber;
run;
proc print data = balance1;
run;
```

* By AccountNumber will only keep one record of accountNumber 2412.

Obs	AccountNumber	Week1	Week4	Balance
1	2412	130	118	12
2	2431	220	198	22
3	2456	173	155	18
4	2477	195	163	32

5.3.2 Using PROC SQL DISTINCT statement

We can get the same result in 5.3.1 using **DISTINCT** statement

```
proc sql;
create table balance2 as
select distinct * from balance;
quit;

proc print data =balance2;
run;
```

Obs	AccountNumber	Week1	Week4	Balance
1	2412	130	118	12
2	2412	135	116	19
3	2431	220	198	22
4	2456	173	155	18
5	2477	195	163	32

This is equivalent to PROC SORT by _all_ in section 5.3.1.

5.4 Most efficient way to obtain duplicate by using first.variable and last.variable

We can get both single and duplicate observations using the following codes.

Let's work on the same original data set in section 5.3.1.

Obs	AccountNumber	Week1	Week4	Balance
1	2412	130	118	12
2	2412	130	118	12
3	2412	135	116	19
4	2431	220	198	22
5	2456	173	155	18
6	2477	195	163	32

```
proc sort data =balance;
by AccountNumber;
run;

data single dup;
  set balance;
  by AccountNumber;
  if first.AccountNumber and last.AccountNumber
    then output single;
  else output dup;
run;
```

Data set single:

Obs	AccountNumber	Week1	Week4	Balance
1	2431	220	198	22
2	2456	173	155	18
3	2477	195	163	32

Data set dup:

Obs	AccountNumber	Week1	Week4	Balance
1	2412	130	118	12
2	2412	130	118	12
3	2412	135	116	19

6. Use array to populate missing value with zero

Original data:

Obs	AccountNumber	Week1	Week4	Balance
1	2412	135	.	.
2	2414	130	121	9
3	2431	.	220	.
4	2456	125	155	-30
5	2477	195	163	32

If there are missing numeric values,we can use the following code to populate missing data
with zero.

```
data test;
  set test;
  array change _numeric_;
    do over change;
      if change=. then change=0;
    end;
run ;
```

We can see that the missing values have been replaced with zero.

Obs	AccountNumber	Week1	Week4	Balance
1	2412	135	0	0
2	2414	130	121	9
3	2431	0	220	0
4	2456	125	155	-30
5	2477	195	163	32

7. Get continuous account membership

Let's say we have a member data with account number, member name, effective date and end date.

We need to figure out how long the account has stayed active. We need to get the continuous membership. In order to get this done, you should have to use the **LAG()** function.

Obs	AccountNum	FirstName	LastName	EffectiveDate	EndDate
1	123	John	H.	05/12/1999	06/30/2002
2	123	John	H.	07/01/2002	06/30/2012
3	123	John	H.	07/01/2012	09/20/2014
4	123	John	H.	09/21/2014	10/30/2019
5	224	Mike	S.	01/05/1999	09/30/2003
6	224	Mike	S.	10/01/2003	09/30/2008
7	224	Mike	S.	11/05/2008	08/10/2012
8	224	Mike	S.	01/05/2015	01/30/2020
9	230	Kate	L.	03/23/1998	03/31/2000
10	230	Kate	L.	04/01/1998	12/31/2010
11	230	Kate	L.	01/01/2011	03/20/2011
12	230	Kate	L.	04/23/2014	10/25/2016

We will have to check the continuity of each account based on effective date and end date. use lag function to get a continuous effective period.

```
proc sort data =member;
by AccountNUm  effectiveDate EndDate;
run;
data member;
set member;
by AccountNUm  effectiveDate EndDate;
retain span(1);
if AccountNum =lag(AccountNUm)  and effectiveDate > lag(EndDate) +1 then span +1;
if first.AccountNum  then span =1;
run;
```

Obs	AccountNum	FirstName	LastName	EffectiveDate	EndDate	span
1	123	John	H.	05/12/1999	06/30/2002	1
2	123	John	H.	07/01/2002	06/30/2012	1
3	123	John	H.	07/01/2012	09/20/2014	1
4	123	John	H.	09/21/2014	10/30/2019	1
5	224	Mike	S.	01/05/1999	09/30/2003	1
6	224	Mike	S.	10/01/2003	09/30/2008	1
7	224	Mike	S.	11/05/2008	08/10/2012	2
8	224	Mike	S.	01/05/2015	01/30/2020	3
9	230	Kate	L.	03/23/1998	03/31/2000	1
10	230	Kate	L.	04/01/1998	12/31/2010	1
11	230	Kate	L.	01/01/2011	03/20/2011	1
12	230	Kate	L.	04/23/2014	10/25/2016	2

In this section, we are going to get the continuity of the effective period including gaps of the dataset with membership data.

```
proc sql;
create table member1 as
select distinct AccountNum, FirstName,LastName, min(effectiveDate) as StartDate format =
date9.,
max(EndDate) as ExpirationDate format = date9.
from member
group by AccountNum, FirstName,LastName,span
order by AccountNum, FirstName,LastName;
quit;

data member1;
set member1;
Days = intck('day',StartDate,ExpirationDate);
Months = intck('month',StartDate,ExpirationDate);
Years = intck('year',StartDate,ExpirationDate);
run;
```

We can see that John H. has been a member for continuous 7476 days and roughly 20 years without any gap. Mike S. has two gaps from 1999 to 2020. One gap is from September,2008 to November,2008. Another gap is from August,2012 to January,2015 about 3 years.

Kate L. has one gap from March 2011 to April 2014.

Obs	AccountNum	FirstName	LastName	StartDate	ExpirationDate	Days	Months	Years
1	123	John	H.	12MAY1999	30OCT2019	7476	245	20
2	224	Mike	S.	05JAN1999	30SEP2008	3556	116	9
3	224	Mike	S.	05NOV2008	10AUG2012	1374	45	4
4	224	Mike	S.	05JAN2015	30JAN2020	1851	60	5
5	230	Kate	L.	23MAR1998	20MAR2011	4745	156	13
6	230	Kate	L.	23APR2014	25OCT2016	916	30	2

8. Dealing with string match

8.1 Using FIND() function to compare two columns either complete or partial

The syntax of FIND() function is:

```
FIND(string, substring <, modifier(s)> <, start-position>)
FIND(string, substring <, start-position> <, modifier(s)>)
```

Modifier and start-position are optional.

Modifier is a character constant, variable, or expression that specifies one or more modifiers.

i or I ignore character cases during the search.

t or T trims trailing blanks from string and substring.

We usually use 'it' together.

Let's create a new data set test with two columns.

```
data test;
  input (Col1   Col2) ($);
  cards;
NC      SE_NCI
CM      CM_AED
SA      SAEF_SUPP
AE      LAB_NCH
AB      ABB_MNCI
AB      KCM_ABE
AB      LSACB_SUPL
;
run;
```

We can use find() function to accomplish the following tasks:

- Compare whether Col2 contains the same string in Col1, we use variable value as an indicator. If value = 1 then it means that Col2 contains the same string in Col1. Otherwise, the value =0.
- Check if Col1 contains character 'A'. If there is a match, then the indicator variable value_A=1. Otherwise, value_A =0.
- Check if Col2 contains a short string 'NC'. A match is found then the indicator variable value_NC=1. Otherwise, value_NC=1.
- Check if Col2 contains a short string 'NC' starting from 5th position of string in Col2. If there is a match, then the indicator variable value_NC5=1. Otherwise, value_NC5=0.

The result of value_NC and value_NC5 are different because the matching starts from the beginning of the string without start-position specified.

```
data test1;
  set test;
  if find(Col2,Col1,'it') then value=1;
  else value=0;

  if find(Col1,'A','it') then value_A=1;
  else value_A=0;

  if find(Col2,'NC','it') then value_NC=1;
  else value_NC=0;

  if find(Col2,'NC','it',5) then value_NC5=1;
  else value_NC5=0;
run;
```

Obs	Col1	Col2	value	value_A	value_NC	value_NC5
1	NC	SE_NCI	1	0	1	0
2	CM	CM_AED	1	0	0	0
3	SA	SAEF_SUP	1	1	0	0
4	AE	LAB_NCH	0	1	1	1
5	AB	ABB_MNCI	1	1	1	1
6	AB	KCM_ABE	1	1	0	0
7	AB	LSACB_SU	0	1	0	0

8.2 Search for one string using INDEX()

You can find a specific character, such as a letter, a group of letters, or special characters, by using the index function.

```
data name_age;
input name $ 1-12 age;
cards;
John Smith  60
Mike Cody   50
Jeff Green  45
James Smith 70
Smith Adams 25
;
run;

proc print data = name_age;
run;
```

Obs	name	age
1	John Smith	60
2	Mike Cody	50
3	Jeff Green	45
4	James Smith	70
5	Smith Adams	25

Let's use the **index** function to find the cases with "Smith" in the name, add a Flag to indicate whether the string is found.

```
data name_age;
set  name_age;
check = index(name, "Smith");
if index(name, "Smith") >0 then Flag =1;
else Flag =0;
run;

proc print data = name_age;
run;
```

We can see that the flag variable has '1' to indicate that the string 'Smith' has been found and '0' to indicate that the string 'Smith' is not found.

Obs	name	age	x	check	Flag
1	John Smith	60	6	6	1
2	Mike Cody	50	0	0	0
3	Jeff Green	45	0	0	0
4	James Smith	70	7	7	1
5	Smith Adams	25	1	1	1

8.3. Check digit or character in a sting

There are two useful functions for checking digits or characters in a string.

The ANYDIGIT function searches a string for the first occurrence of any character that is a digit. If such a character is found, ANYDIGIT returns the position in the string of that character. If no such character is found, ANYDIGIT returns a value of 0.

The ANYALPHA function searches a string for the first occurrence of any character that is an uppercase or lowercase letter. If such a character is found, ANYALPHA returns the position in the string of that character. If no such character is found, ANYALPHA returns a value of 0.

If a string has no character or any alphabet then ANYALPHA() will return 0.
If a string has no digit at all then ANYDIGIT() will return 0.

Let's look at the dataset **TEST**:

```
data TEST;
input (Col1 Col2) ($);
cards;
NC SE_NCI
CM CM_12
SA SAEF_SUPP
AE 23456
AB A3424.36
AB KC3M_ABE
AB L2389.701
;
run;

proc print data = TEST; run;
```

Obs	Col1	Col2
1	NC	SE_NCI
2	CM	CM_12
3	SA	SAEF_SUP
4	AE	23456
5	AB	A3424.36
6	AB	KC3M_ABE
7	AB	L2389.70

We add four new variables:

alphabet_flag_Col1
alphabet_flag_Col2
digit_flag_Col1
digit_flag_Col12

```
data FLAG;
set TEST;
alphabet_flag_Col1 = anyalpha(Col1);
alphabet_flag_Col2 = anyalpha(Col2);
digit_flag_Col1 = anydigit(Col1);
digit_flag_Col2 = anydigit(Col2);
run;
proc print data = FLAG; run;
```

We can see that digit_flag_Col1 has 0 for all observations and alphabet_flag_Col2 has one 0 for observation 4. The digit_Col2 contains the position numbers of any digit in the string.

Obs	Col1	Col2	alphabet_flag_Col1	alphabet_flag_Col2	digit_flag_Col1	digit_flag_Col2
1	NC	SE_NCI	1	1	0	0
2	CM	CM_12	1	1	0	4
3	SA	SAEF_SUP	1	1	0	0
4	AE	23456	1	0	0	1
5	AB	A3424.36	1	1	0	2
6	AB	KC3M_ABE	1	1	0	3
7	AB	L2389.70	1	1	0	2

8.4 Use PRXMATCH in place of multiple INDEX functions

If you need to search a character variable for multiple different substrings, the conventional method is to link several INDEX function calls together with OR conditions:

```
if index(lowcase(charvar),'this') > 0 or
   index(lowcase(charvar),'that') > 0 or
   index(lowcase(charvar),'other') > 0 then found = 1;
else found=0;
```

The PRXMATCH function, for Perl Regular Expressions Match, can do it all in a single call.

This requires less typing and fewer chances for mistakes:

```
if prxmatch("m/this|that|other/oi",charvar) > 0 then found=1;
else found=0;
```

Chapter 10

Basic statistical procedures

When we have the clean data, the basic thing we do is to describe data. In this chapter we are going to go through several fundamental procedures.

1. Using proc means

We can get basic statistics such as mean, median, standard deviation, minimum, maximum, 95% confidence interval

```
FILENAME REFFILE '/home/project/Client_hw.xls';

PROC IMPORT DATAFILE=REFFILE
      DBMS=XLS
      OUT= WORK.HW;
      GETNAMES=YES;
RUN;

PROC CONTENTS DATA=WORK.HW; RUN;

PROC MEANS DATA = HW  N MEAN MEDIAN STDDEV CLM MIN MAX
                      SUM VAR Q1 Q3  MAXDEC =2 ;
RUN;
```

Alphabetic List of Variables and Attributes						
#	Variable	Type	Len	Format	Informat	Label
3	Age	Num	8	BEST11.		Age
1	CaseNumber	Num	8	BEST11.		CaseNumber
2	Gender	Char	11	$11.	$11.	Gender
4	Height	Num	8	BEST11.		Height
5	Weight	Num	8	BEST11.		Weight

Variable	Label	N	Mean	Median	Std Dev	Lower 95% CL for Mean	Upper 95% CL for Mean	Minimum	Maximum	Sum	Variance	Lower Quartile	Upper Quartile
CaseNumber	CaseNumber	14	7.50	7.50	4.18	5.08	9.92	1.00	14.00	105.00	17.50	4.00	11.00
Age	Age	14	60.29	63.00	17.56	50.14	70.43	21.00	82.00	844.00	308.53	49.00	74.00
Height	Height	14	58.57	59.00	4.54	55.95	61.19	49.00	65.00	820.00	20.57	58.00	62.00
Weight	Weight	14	191.93	192.50	49.86	163.14	220.71	110.00	304.00	2687.00	2485.61	155.00	215.00

You can use **BY** statement to run the procedure to get the statistics of the **BY** variable. Remember to always sort the data set first by the same BY variable. You can also use the **CLASS** statement.

```
PROC SORT DATA = HW;
BY Gender;
RUN;

PROC MEANS DATA = HW  N MEAN MEDIAN STDDEV CLM MIN MAX SUM VAR
                Q1 Q3 MAXDEC =2 ;
BY GENDER;
RUN;

PROC MEANS DATA = HW  N MEAN MEDIAN STDDEV CLM MIN MAX SUM VAR
                Q1 Q3 MAXDEC =2 ;
BY GENDER;
RUN;
```

We can get the statistics for males and females.

Gender	N Obs	Variable	Label	N	Mean	Median	Std Dev	Lower 95% CL for Mean	Upper 95% CL for Mean	Minimum	Maximum	Sum	Variance	Lower Quartile	Upper Quartile
F	5	CaseNumber	CaseNumber	5	8.40	9.00	5.13	2.03	14.77	1.00	14.00	42.00	26.30	6.00	12.00
		Age	Age	5	63.40	62.00	5.18	56.97	69.83	59.00	72.00	317.00	26.80	60.00	64.00
		Height	Height	5	56.80	58.00	6.10	49.23	64.37	49.00	65.00	284.00	37.20	53.00	59.00
		Weight	Weight	5	192.20	203.00	25.19	160.92	223.48	155.00	215.00	961.00	634.70	178.00	210.00
M	9	CaseNumber	CaseNumber	9	7.00	7.00	3.81	4.07	9.93	2.00	13.00	63.00	14.50	4.00	10.00
		Age	Age	9	58.56	64.00	21.88	41.74	75.37	21.00	82.00	527.00	478.53	40.00	75.00
		Height	Height	9	59.56	60.00	3.43	56.92	62.19	52.00	63.00	536.00	11.78	58.00	62.00
		Weight	Weight	9	191.78	189.00	61.01	144.88	238.67	110.00	304.00	1726.00	3721.69	146.00	223.00

2. Using PROC UNIVARIATE

If you want a more extensive list of statistics, such as tests of normality, probability plots, box plot, **PROC UNIVARIATE** is the best way to go.

```
FILENAME REFFILE '/home/project/Client_hw.xls';


PROC IMPORT DATAFILE=REFFILE
     DBMS=XLS
     OUT= HW;
     GETNAMES=YES;
RUN;

PROC CONTENTS DATA = HW; RUN;


PROC MEANS DATA = HW  N MEAN MEDIAN STDDEV CLM MIN MAX SUM VAR Q1 Q3
MAXDEC =2 ;
RUN;


PROC UNIVARIATE DATA = HW   NORMAL PLOT;
VAR AGE ;
HISTOGRAM AGE;
RUN;
```

The UNIVARIATE Procedure
Variable: Age (Age)

Moments			
N	15	Sum Weights	15
Mean	60.0666667	Sum Observations	901
Std Deviation	16.9472571	Variance	287.209524
Skewness	-0.8162015	Kurtosis	0.54665039
Uncorrected SS	58141	Corrected SS	4020.93333
Coeff Variation	28.2140796	Std Error Mean	4.37576297

Basic Statistical Measures			
Location		Variability	
Mean	60.06667	Std Deviation	16.94726
Median	62.00000	Variance	287.20952
Mode	40.00000	Range	61.00000
		Interquartile Range	25.00000

Tests for Normality				
Test	Statistic		p Value	
Shapiro-Wilk	W	0.936643	Pr < W	0.3420
Kolmogorov-Smirnov	D	0.161535	Pr > D	>0.1500
Cramer-von Mises	W-Sq	0.055077	Pr > W-Sq	>0.2500
Anderson-Darling	A-Sq	0.354298	Pr > A-Sq	>0.2500

Quantiles (Definition 5)	
Level	Quantile
100% Max	82
99%	82
95%	82
90%	82
75% Q3	74
50% Median	62
25% Q1	49
10%	40
5%	21
1%	21
0% Min	21

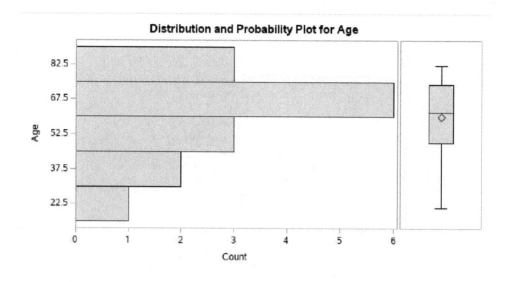

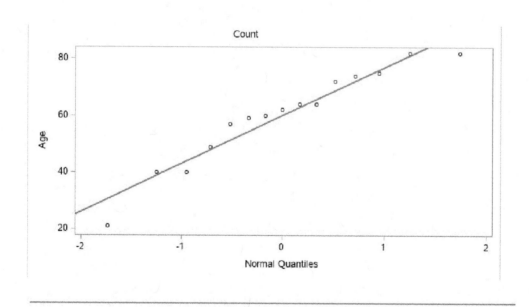

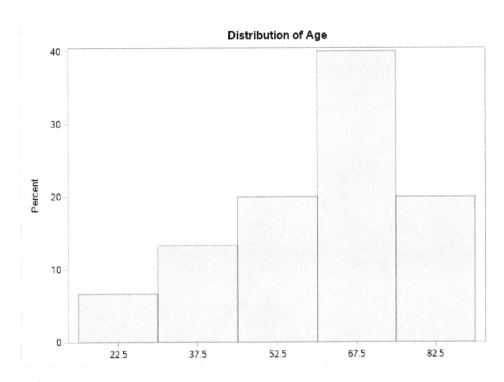

Distribution of Age

Similarly, you can also use **CLASS** statement for **PROC UNIVARIATE** to get the statistics and plots for **CLASS** variables.

```
PROC UNIVARIATE DATA = HW   NORMAL PLOT;
CLASS GENDER;
VAR AGE ;
HISTOGRAM AGE;
RUN;
```

The UNIVARIATE Procedure
Variable: Age (Age)
Gender = F

Moments			
N	5	Sum Weights	5
Mean	63.4	Sum Observations	317
Std Deviation	5.17687164	Variance	26.8
Skewness	1.52875707	Kurtosis	2.41172867
Uncorrected SS	20205	Corrected SS	107.2
Coeff Variation	8.16541268	Std Error Mean	2.31516738

Basic Statistical Measures			
Location		Variability	
Mean	63.40000	Std Deviation	5.17687
Median	62.00000	Variance	26.80000
Mode	.	Range	13.00000
		Interquartile Range	4.00000

The UNIVARIATE Procedure
Variable: Age (Age)
Gender = F

Moments			
N	5	Sum Weights	5
Mean	63.4	Sum Observations	317
Std Deviation	5.17687164	Variance	26.8
Skewness	1.52875707	Kurtosis	2.41172867
Uncorrected SS	20205	Corrected SS	107.2
Coeff Variation	8.16541268	Std Error Mean	2.31516738

Basic Statistical Measures			
Location		Variability	
Mean	63.40000	Std Deviation	5.17687
Median	62.00000	Variance	26.80000
Mode	.	Range	13.00000
		Interquartile Range	4.00000

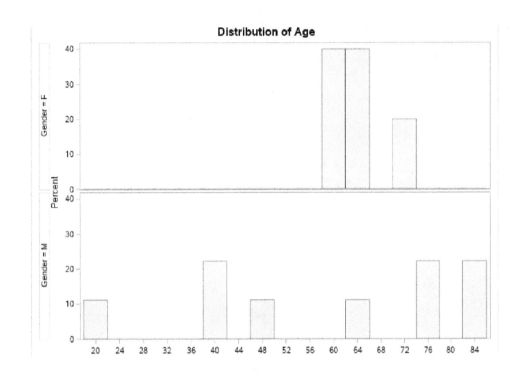

Distribution of Age

3. Bar Graphs

We can use **PROC GCHART** to get bar graphs on frequency.

```
FILENAME REFFILE '/home/llll12river/project/Client_hw.xls';
PROC IMPORT DATAFILE=REFFILE
     DBMS=XLS
     OUT= HW;
     GETNAMES=YES;
RUN;
PROC GCHART DATA = HW;
VAR WEIGHT;
RUN;
```

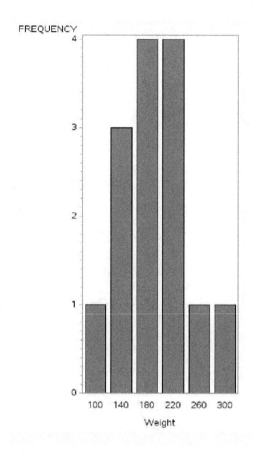

4. Plotting Data

We can investigate the relationship between height and weight in the HW data set by using

PROC PLOT statement

```
PROC PLOT DATA = HW;
Title "Using Gender to Generate the Plotting Symbol";
PLOT WEIGHT*HEIGHT ;
RUN;
```

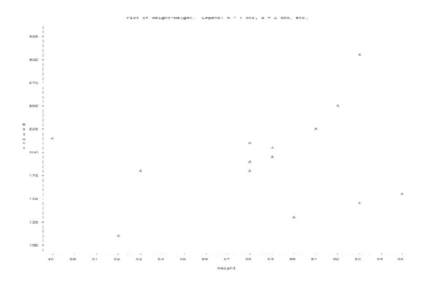

We can use the following codes to generate graphs for males and females separately on the same plot.

```
PROC PLOT DATA = HW1;
Title "Using Gender to Generate the Plotting Symbol";
PLOT WEIGHT*HEIGHT = GENDER;
RUN;
```

5. Using PROC FREQ to get frequency

We can use the PROC FREQ statement to calculate the frequency of categorical variables. Let's see how many males and females there are in our sample data HW.

```
FILENAME REFFILE '/home/llll12river/project/Client_hw.xls';
PROC IMPORT DATAFILE=REFFILE
      DBMS=XLS
      OUT= HW;
      GETNAMES=YES;
RUN;

PROC FREQ DATA = HW;
TABLE GENDER;
RUN;
```

The FREQ Procedure

Gender				
Gender	Frequency	Percent	Cumulative Frequency	Cumulative Percent
F	6	40.00	6	40.00
M	9	60.00	15	100.00

6. Two sample t- test

Two sample t-test is most commonly used when we compare two independent samples.

Two sample t-test assumes that

1.   There is one continuous dependent variable and one categorical independent variable (with 2 levels);

2.   The two samples are independent;

3.   The two samples follow normal distributions

Let's compare the height between the males and females in our sample.

```
FILENAME REFFILE '/home/llll12river/project/Client_hw.xls';

PROC IMPORT DATAFILE=REFFILE
     DBMS=XLS
     OUT= HW;
     GETNAMES=YES;
RUN;

PROC TTEST DATA = HW ;
   TITLE "Two sample t-test example";
   CLASS GENDER;
   VAR HEIGHT;
RUN;
```

Two sample t-test example

The TTEST Procedure

Variable: Height (Height)

Gender	Method	N	Mean	Std Dev	Std Err	Minimum	Maximum
F		5	56.8000	6.0992	2.7276	49.0000	65.0000
M		9	59.5556	3.4319	1.1440	52.0000	63.0000
Diff (1-2)	Pooled		-2.7556	4.5002	2.5101		
Diff (1-2)	Satterthwaite		-2.7556		2.9578		

Gender	Method	Mean	95% CL Mean		Std Dev	95% CL Std Dev	
F		56.8000	49.2269	64.3731	6.0992	3.6542	17.5263
M		59.5556	56.9176	62.1935	3.4319	2.3181	6.5747
Diff (1-2)	Pooled	-2.7556	-8.2246	2.7135	4.5002	3.2270	7.4286
Diff (1-2)	Satterthwaite	-2.7556	-10.1751	4.6640			

Method	Variances	DF	t Value	Pr > |t|
Pooled	Equal	12	-1.10	0.2938
Satterthwaite	Unequal	5.4466	-0.93	0.3910

Equality of Variances				
Method	Num DF	Den DF	F Value	Pr > F
Folded F	4	8	3.16	0.1559

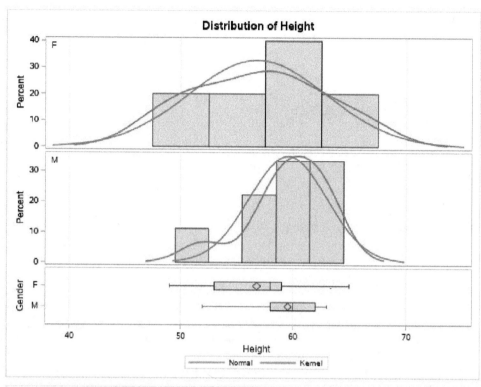

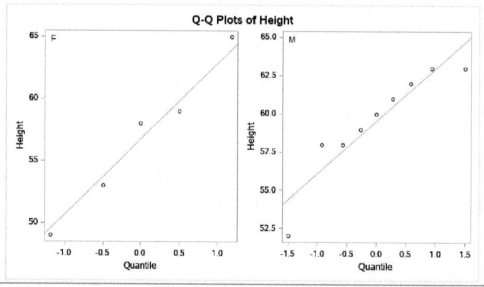

Chapter 11

Data management and automation setup

It is very practical that some of our SAS programs need to run repeatedly over time. There are many ways to set up the automation process. Here we just give a few simple examples.

1. X statement and batch file

The X statement is a powerful statement that comes with Base SAS and allows you to issue OS commands as part of a SAS program or interactively during a SAS session. This gives you the power to perform many actions in the SAS environment.

1. 1 Delete and copy file in your folder

```
x   "del  C:\yourdirectory\yourMe.txt";

x "copy  C:\yourdirectory1\yourMe.txt  C:\yourdirectory2\yourMe.txt ";
```

1.2 Creating Batch file in SAS using data_ null_ in run time

We can use a batch file which will be able to run more complicated codes directly in the window command line environment through SAS.

Now we are going to create a SAS file which will copy and rename files from one folder to another folder.

Step1: Open a txt file then save as with extension .bat : For example, YouBatch.bat

Step2: Run the following codes to write command line to the existing batch file

```
%let dt = %sysfunc(PUTN(%eval(%sysfunc(date())-2),yymmddn8.));

%macro rename(file1=,dir2 =,file2=,dir1=,dt1=&dt);

data _null_;

file "C:\your directory1\YourBatch.bat";

put " COPY  &dir2\&file2&dt1...csv   &dir1\&file1..csv "/

"exit";

run;

x "C:\your directory1\YourBatch.bat";

%mend;

%rename(file1= name1 ,dir2 = d2   ,file2=name2, dir1=, dt1=&dt);
```

The above codes copy all CSV files from folder dir2 to folder dir1.

1.3 Create a batch file for automation

We can create a batch file to contain multiple SAS programming files and schedule the batch file to run in any task scheduler, such MicroSoft task scheduler.
In order to do this, we will follow the two steps:
Step1: Open a txt file then save as with extension .bat : For example, YouBatchTest.bat

Step2: Copy the following codes to the existing batch file and save log file to the folder 'C:\Program Files \log'

```
C:\Program Files\SAS\SAS9.4\sas.exe" -sysin C:\Code\program1.sas  -log  C:\Program
Files \log
```

C:\Program Files\SAS\SAS9.4\sas.exe" -sysin C:\Code\program2.sas -log C:\Program Files \log

C:\Program Files\SAS\SAS9.4\sas.exe" -sysin C:\Code\program3.sas -log C:\Program Files \log

We can schedule an automation job to run our batch test file (YouBatchTest.bat), which will run the sas program1,program2 and program3. Three log files will be generated in   the folder C:\Program Files \log.

The log files provide us the opportunity to check errors if any occurs in the run time. We can also run sas code to check errors automatically, which will improve the program efficiency. Please refer to section **4. Check log file for errors** for details in this chapter.

1.4 Check file existence and send reminder email if file is not there

Use **fileexist()** function to check files.

```
%let dt = %sysfunc(PUTN(%eval(%sysfunc(date())-2),yymmddn8.));

%let d2 = C:\your directory;

%let d1 = C:\your directory4 ;

%put &dt &d1,&d2;

*checkfile;
%macro checkfile(file1=,dir2 =,file2=,dir1=,dt1=&dt);

%if %sysfunc(fileexist(&dir2\&file2&dt1...csv )) %then

      %do ;

      data _null_;

      file "C:\your directory1\YourBatch.bat";

      put " COPY " """&dir2\&file2&&dt1...csv""" " &dir1\&file1..csv "/
```

```
        "exit";

      run;

    x "C:\your directory1\YourBatch.bat";

      %end;

%else %do;

*Send email if the file doesn't exist.
Compile email message file;

data _null_;

  file "C:\message\YourEmailMessage.txt";

  put " Add email content1   "/

      "email content12"/;

run;

*send email message and attachment file;

data _null_;

file "C:\batch\YourTransitionFile.bat" lrecl=2000;

put "set msgfile=C:\message\YourEmailMessage.txt"/

    'set emsubject=" Your email subject "'/

    'set emmail= Your email'/

    "blat %msgfile% -from Your email -to %emmail% -subject %emsubject% "/

    "exit";

run;

x "C:\batch\YourTransitionFile.bat"; run;

%end;
```

%mend;

%checkfile(file1=Correspondence,dir2 =&d2,   file2=Correspondence_, dir1 =&d1);

1.5. Copy and Rename csv files;


```
%macro rename(file1=,dir2 =,file2=,dir1=,dt1=&dt);

data _null_;

file "C:\your directory1\YourBatch.bat";

put " COPY  &dir2\&file2&dt1...csv   &dir1\&file1..csv "/

"exit";

run;

x "C:\your directory1\YourBatch.bat";

%mend;


%rename(file1=ACG_Custom, dir2 =&d2,     file2=ACG_Custom_ , dir1 =&d1 );


* The SAS program will pause for 3 minutes;

Data _null_;

sleep_time = Sleep(180,1);

run;
```

2. Loop through all files in one directory

2.1. Loop through a list

You can print out each of the 5 alphabets using the following codes.

```
%let list = a b c d e;

%macro loop(vlist=);

%let nwords=%sysfunc(countw(&vlist.));

%do i=1 %to &nwords;

%put %scan(&vlist, &i);

%end;

%mend;

%loop(vlist =&list);
```

2.2 Get file list

In the following example, we are going to get a file list for the last 45 CSV data files .

```
%macro file(dir1 =,file1=,dir2 =);

filename DIRLIST pipe "dir /B &dir2\*.csv";

 data filelist ;
    length fname $256;
    infile dirlist length=reclen ;
```

```
  input fname $varying256. reclen ;
    order=_n_;
    filename = compress("&d2\"|| substr(fname,1,length(fname)-0));
 run;



*Get the last 45 files;

 %let obswant = 45;

data filelist1 (keep = filename);
set filelist  nobs=obscount;
if _n_ gt (obscount-&&obswant.);
run;


proc export data = filelist1
outfile = "&dir2\list.txt"
dbms = tab replace;
PUTNAMES=NO;
run;

%mend;

%file(dir1 =dir1,file1=file1,dir2 =dir2);
```

3. Archive multiple files

We always have to archive files to release the storage space on the server. One of the ways to do this is to zip up files , and in the meantime to delete old files. Please be aware that we have to be extremely careful when deleting files. We have to make sure the files are really not needed in the future.

3.1 Zip multiple CSV files

```
%let dt = %sysfunc(PUTN(%eval(%sysfunc(date())-4),yymmddn8.));

%put &dt;

%macro zipfile(dir1 =,file1=,dir2 =,file2=,dt1=&dt);

data _null_;

file "C:\your directory1\YourBatch.bat";
put '"C:\Program Files\winzip\wzzip" ' "&dir1\&file1..zip &dir2\&file2&dt1...csv"/
"del &dir2\&file2&dt1...csv"/
"exit";

run;

x "C:\your directory1\YourBatch.bat";

%mend;

 %zipfile(dir1 =C:\your directory\archive,file1=Custom,dir2 =C:\your directory,
file2=Custom);




 *unzip files
*unzip the current zip file to corresponding folder;

%macro unzipfile(dir1 =,file1=,dir2 =,file2=);

data _null_;
file "C:\your directory1\YourBatch.bat";
put  '"C:\Program Files\winzip\wzunzip" ' """"&dir1\&file1..zip"""" ' """"&dir2\"""/
"exit" ;
run;
```

```
x "C:\your directory1\YourBatch.bat";

%mend;


 %unzipfile(dir1 =C:\your directory\archive,file1=Custom,dir2 =C:\your directory,
file2=Custom);
```

3.2 Delete multiple data files in archive

```
%macro Clean_archive();

data _null_;

file "C:\your directory1\YourBatch.bat";

put

"del C:\your directory\archive\oldfile1.zip"/      /* delete one zip file*/

"del C:\your directory\archive\oldfile2.csv"/     /* delete one CSV  file*/

"del C:\your directory\archive\unwanted\*.csv"/   /*delete ALL CSV files in unwanted folder*/

"exit";

run;

x "C:\your directory1\YourBatch.bat";

%mend;

%Clean_archive();
```

3.3 If data exist then replace with new data

```
%macro copyFiles(dir=C:\your directory2);

%let filrf=FileList;

%let rc=%sysfunc(filename(filrf,"&dir"));

%let did=%sysfunc(dopen(&filrf));

%let memcount=%sysfunc(dnum(&did));

%put &memcount;

%if (&memcount > 0) %then %do;

data _null_;

file "C:\your directory1\YourBatch.bat";

put  "COPY C:\your directory2\* C:\your directory3\ "/

"exit";

run;

x "C:\your directory1\YourBatch.bat";

%end;

%let rcls=%sysfunc(dclose(&did));

run;

%mend ;

%copyFiles();
```

4. Check log file for errors

* Check log file

```
%let subdir= C:\log\;

%let out= C:\Log\log_errors.xlsx;

 filename dir pipe "dir &subdir.*.log /B";

data new;

 infile dir truncover;

 /* Read a log file from the subdirectory*/

 input filename $3000.;

 filename="&subdir" || filename;

 length lname logfile $2000;

  infile dummy filevar=filename filename=lname end=done truncover;

 do while (not done);

   /* Read a record from the log file*/

  input Text $5. @;

  if Text =:'ERROR:' then do;

   input @6 msg $76.;

   logfile=lname;

   output;

   end;
```

```sas
      else input;

      end;

run;



/* create the report */

proc export data = new

outfile = "&out"

dbms =xlsx label replace;

run;


data _NULL_;

      if 0 then set .new nobs=n;

      call symputx('numobs',n);

      stop;

run;

%put nobs=&numobs;


%macro execute;

%if %eval(&numobs)>0 %then %do;

data _null_;

  file "message.txt";
```

```
    put " Email contents"/

        "more content,"/;

run;

*send email message;

data _null_;

file "C:\YourTransitionFile.bat" lrecl=2000;

put "set msgfile=C:\message\YourEmailMessage.txt"/

    'set emsubject="Log files with errors"'/

    "set emattach=&out"/

    'set emmail=Your email,Other email'/

    "blat %msgfile% -from Your email -to %emmail% -subject %emsubject% -attach
%emattach%"/

    "exit";

run;


x "C:\YourTransitionFile.bat"; run;

%end;

%mend;

%execute;
```

Tip: If you save the above log file as LogCheck.sas, then you can put the file at the very end of your batch file for automation, which you have created in section **1.3** . The macro program %execute will collect all log errors into excel file log_errors.xlsx. It will be an easy task to find the errors for multiple sas programs.

Here is the example:

```
C:\Program Files\SAS\SAS9.4\sas.exe" -sysin C:\Code\program1.sas   -log  C:\Program
Files \log

C:\Program Files\SAS\SAS9.4\sas.exe" -sysin C:\Code\program2.sas   -log  C:\Program
Files \log

C:\Program Files\SAS\SAS9.4\sas.exe" -sysin C:\Code\program3.sas   -log  C:\Program
Files \log

C:\Program Files\SAS\SAS9.4\sas.exe" -sysin C:\Code\ LogCheck.sas  -log
C:\Program Files \log
```

5. Create user defined function

In the following example,we created a user defined function (**networkdays()**) in SAS.
The function is to calculate the work days /business days with consideration of excluding weekend, holiday and company floating holidays.

```
libname a 'C:\Function';
* work day function: NETWORKDAYS ;
proc fcmp  outlib=a.myfuncs.dates;
  function networkdays(d1,d2,holidayDataset $,dateColumn $);
    /* make sure the start date < end date */
      start_date = min(d1,d2);
      end_date = max(d1,d2);
    /* read holiday data into array */
    /* array will resize as necessary */
      array holidays[1] / nosymbols;
    if (not missing(holidayDataset) and exist(holidayDataset)) then
      rc = read_array(holidayDataset, holidays, dateColumn);
    *else put "NOTE: networkdays(): No Holiday data considered";

    /* INTCK computes transitions from one day to the next */
```

```
   /* To include the start date, if it is a weekday, then */
    /*  make the start date one day earlier.              */
   /*  if (1 < weekday(start_date)< 7) then
        calc_start_date = start_date-1;
      else  */
        calc_start_date = start_date;
        diff = intck('WEEKDAY', calc_start_date, end_date);
        do i = 1 to dim(holidays);
        if (1 < weekday(holidays[i])< 7) and
        (start_date <= holidays[i] <= end_date) then
             diff = diff - 1;
      end;
      return(diff);
   endsub;
run; quit;

    /* Make a call from the DATA step. */
option cmplib = (a.myfuncs.dates);

/*This function can read a range of holiday dates from a data set.
you could use the function like the following example:*/

data a.holiday_test;
   length HOLIDAYDATE 8;
   format HOLIDAYDATE date9.;
   infile datalines dsd;
   input HOLIDAYDATE: date9.;
datalines;
04JUL2019
01JAN2019
25DEC2019
01JAN2020
;
run;


data test2;
   length chardate1 $10
          chardate2 $10;
   infile datalines;
   input chardate1 $
      chardate2 $;
   date1 = input(chardate1,DATE9.);
   date2 = input(chardate2,DATE9.);
   FORMAT   date1 date9. date2 date9.;
datalines;
10SEP2018  10OCT2018
09SEP2019  20SEP2019
03JUL2019  11JUL2019
19SEP2020  26SEP2020
;
run;
```

```
proc print data = test2;
run;
proc contents data =  test2;
run;
data test3;
set test2;
  workdays = networkdays(date1, date2, "work.holidaytest","holidaydate");
   if workdays <=10 then resolvedWithin10Days=1;
  else resolvedWithin10Days=0;
run;

proc print data = test3;
run;
```

chardate1	chardate2	date1	date2	workdays	resolvedWithin10Days
10SEP2018	10OCT2018	10SEP2018	10OCT2018	22	0
09SEP2019	20SEP2019	09SEP2019	20SEP2019	9	1
03JUL2019	11JUL2019	03JUL2019	11JUL2019	6	1
19SEP2020	26SEP2020	19SEP2020	26SEP2020	5	1

Reference

www.sas.com

https://support.sas.com/software/products/ondemand-academics

Author's Note

Hope you find this book useful for your programming. I enjoy all feedback from readers. If you would like to comment on this book, please post a review on Amazon. You can also reach the author at email: llll12river@gmail.com

Thanks for reading!

Lillian Ren